4 |10
1 00

Loving
Relationships

The only way to have a perfect relationship
is to have
two people
experiencing their own perfection.

Leonard Orr

Loving Relationships

The Secrets of a Great Relationship

Sondra Ray

creator of
The Loving Relationships Training

CELESTIALARTS

Berkeley, California

Text design and typography by HMS Typography, Inc.
Cover design by Sarah Levin
Cover illustration by Beth Bonart

FIRST CELESTIAL ARTS PRINTING 1980

Library of Congress Cataloging in Publication Data

Ray, Sondra
    Loving relationships

        1. Interpersonal relations.   2. Love.
3. Friendship   4. Self-acceptance.   I. Title
HM132.R29   302.3'4   79-55633
ISBN 0-89087-244-9

23 24 25 26 - 98 97 96

DEDICATION

I dedicate this book to Shri Shri 1008 Shri
Bhagwan Herakhan Wale Baba, The Yogi Christ of India,
who teaches me what I need to know, who helps me teach what I know,
who guides me eternally, and who gives me this supremely wonderful,
most important relationship.

Om Namaha Shivai

May everything I write be something beautiful for God

The reason this book is different from other books you may have read on relationships is because it is based on the following:

1. The spiritual truth that THOUGHT IS CREATIVE and that you can change anything by changing your thoughts, especially how to change the deep subconscious thoughts that are destructive to relationships;

2. New research from the effects of Birth Trauma. This information was never really available before. Rebirthing, a process that heals the damage done physically and psychologically at birth, came about five years ago and has clearly taught us how your birth affects your relationships;

3. The concept of Physical Immortality—learning how to master your body so that you can actually start "Youthing" and keep your body any age you wish. This means you can prolong your life as long as you like once you master the philosophy, continue Rebirthing, and change your thoughts.

Because of these spiritual truths and the fact that we are now entering the true age of enlightenment, ours may be the first generation in which relationships work in such a way that they bring us total healing and aliveness.

Contents

Relationships From Now On

There have always been perfect, truthful, deep, satisfying, and exciting relationships in the world, but they have been extremely rare and usually of short duration. Romantic literature described a longed-for ideal relationship that was intense, spontaneous, which overcame all initial obstacles, and which had one of two possible endings: either the lovers died a mutual death at the height of their passion (Tristan and Isolde, Romeo and Juliet), thus preserving and immortalizing the intensity of their commitment; or, they "lived happily ever after" (Grimm's Fairy Tales), after which statement the account ceases in order not to depress the reader with the mundane details and daily, repetitious circumstances of "married life." These were the models which most people were given while growing up. These ideals created the hope and the struggle which blinded us to how relationships actually work and to what the underlying fundamental principles of love and friendship between people really are.

The last thirty years in the United States have seen the breaking of patterns of thought about the way relationships should be. Divorce increased tremendously, and it was clear that the old ways wouldn't work so well for the new people. The Sexual Revolution became integrated into a new morality that still lacks a form that will provide real, lasting satisfaction. The multiplicity of lifestyles from which we can choose is bewildering. Yet the insights which can give you power over your own life and allow you to clear up whatever is not satisfying in your experience are the truths of life itself, and are not special to any life*style*. This book is about those truths, and understanding them will show the way to bring light, freedom, power, and true satisfaction through love to any form of relationship that you may choose.

The "truths" are old; they have always existed, but seldom have been seen clearly. Intuitive, healthy people simply demonstrated them by being able to say what was in their hearts and living together without possessiveness. The LRT (Loving Relationships Training, or Life-as-Relationship Training) has brought these principles together in a thorough, easy-to-understand, exciting experience that leaves you no longer able to pretend you didn't get it. If your relationship breaks down, you'll know how to find out why it did and what to do about it. This book, and the training behind it, marks the end of rigidity, suppression, and false purposes in human relationships. It provides the foundation for a growth of understanding among large masses of people of what they have always wanted and how to have it in their lives now.

The group of friends which exists around and through the LRT expands daily, with or without the training. Those of us who have been especially close to Sondra and to each other through our participation as trainers are taking these ideas to higher and higher levels of energy and experience in our relationships with each other. We trust and love each other with no tolerance for untruths. Outwardly, there may at times appear to be nothing unusual about us; inwardly, the trust and mutual acknowledgment are profoundly satisfying, nourishing, and healing.

As you read this book, enter into relationship with Sondra and her friends. We *live* this book, and if you find us through these pages we will receive you into our lives with joy.

Fred Lehrman

Introduction

The Loving Relationships Training (LRT) was created so that you can fully love yourself and experience an abundance of love and joy in all your relationships all of the time. This book contains many ideas from the Training and is intended to help you heal yourself in your present relationships and to clear your mind right now on the whole subject of relationships. When you understand the Loving Relationships Training, you will probably want to allow yourself the wonderful experience of healing through sharing the processes and enjoying the energies of other people like yourself.

The first step, always, is to heal ourselves. It is my intention to help you do that easily, effortlessly. We teach what we need to learn. I needed to learn about relationships and so I created the LRT. I was so determined to master relationships that I was going to give the training to myself whether anyone else came or not. In the beginning it didn't matter to me if I had one student or one hundred, I just wanted to get it. The information kept coming through me and I kept writing it down. At times I had to take the training from other trainers in order to get it myself. I love it and I'm thrilled to share it.

Now let's get right down to it. The secrets of a great relationship are right there in the table of contents of this book. When you read that page, you may tend to think it sounds too hard, or that it will take too long. If you want to make it hard, that is up to you. I suggest you make it fun and easy.

It will certainly be more fun and much easier to accomplish these things than it is to hang on to old negative patterns that are killing you. Furthermore, when you do give up old patterns by doing the processes explained in this book, you will find that your own vital energy is naturally released. Feeling energetic and positive, you will certainly have more fun.

If you have a struggle pattern, however, you might find yourself struggling even more. Most people have a pattern of struggling that began with their struggle to be born and they have retained the unconscious thought "Life is a struggle." (Fortunately new methods of birth are preventing this today, and the Rebirthing process is healing the adults who had traumatic births.)

To begin, please meditate on this affirmation: *By following the simple instructions in this book, I am releasing old patterns effortlessly and joyfully and I can have really great relationships that heal me.*

You will be so relieved to have this information that you will actually feel your body come alive and get turned on. That is what happens when you let go of fears such as "There is no way that relationship can work for me" or "I'll never get what I want in a loving relationship."

There is another truth I want to give you right now. It would be impossible to transfer the real heart of the Training onto the pages of a book. Physically and emotionally experiencing the energy of the LRT is what transforms the people who take it. The immense amount of energy and love in the room pushes anything unlike love out of the people and out of the space. They come out of the Training able to receive a lot more love because the blocks to receiving are gone. They learn how to handle pleasure as they are immersed in a tremendous amount of energy. (Never have I felt this amount of energy and movement elsewhere, except with Babaji, the Yogi Christ of India, or in a particularly intense Rebirthing.)

Your willingness to read this book is a sure sign that you are ready for the Training.

Because you are willing to receive this much of the Source,

good things will start happening to you immediately. Be assured that just your thinking "I am now willing to look at my life and relationships and clean them up" will begin a magical transformation. Tell yourself "I might even take the LRT and get Rebirthed." People often report that as soon as they sign up for the Training, their relationships start improving. The reason for this is quite simple: You are ready.

If we all continue to master this together, how exciting it will be to live together in all the positive energy!
more fully realizing my own perfection.

People with me are always in the Training. So it had better be fun! And it is. One graduate, Peter, started the rumor that it is "Heaven on Earth." It is heaven to me, because I seem to channel the most perfect thoughts during Training. Heaven is not a place, you know; it is the realm of perfect ideas.

That is why the first day of the Training is devoted to powerful processes that clear away the garbage of consciousness that gets in the way of a person's experiencing his or her own perfection.

I created the Training to heal myself. It has become so easy to share, that now people are getting healed along with me. Isn't that what we all want? To feel healed in body, mind, and spirit and to be excited about life?

The world is meant to be a playground where we all have fun doing every little thing we do.

I wanted to acknowledge those people who came before me and started the healing of mass consciousness. And I want to acknowledge myself for searching for the Truth for years and not giving up until I found it.

I love you.

Sondra Ray!

Attracting a Mate

It is very easy to attract a mate or anyone if you think that you can! If you understand a little metaphysics, the days of worrying and hoping and looking in singles bars are over. There is such a thing as the "Universal Metaphysical Law of Attraction." I prefer to call it *The Cosmic Dating Service*. It always works too, if you let it. You don't have to worry about the where or the how. The person you are looking for will show up *anywhere*, when and only when you are ready. You merely have to think the right thoughts and let go of any resistance you have to receiving.

The mistake that most people make is forgetting that their thoughts produce results *all the time*. People walk around thinking things like "I'll never find anybody" or "There aren't any available men (or women) around here." or "Nobody ever asks me out," and then they wonder why they are home alone! Especially after there is a breakup, the person "left behind" usually ends up thinking something like "I'll never find anyone as good as him (or her)," "I'll never make it alone," or "My life is over." All of these thoughts are destructive and produce negative results.

It is important to keep your heart open to receive. Then it is a matter of accepting and being certain that you deserve what you want. A good affirmation is "I am now willing to let into my life the man (or woman) I desire." If you do not get a result after saying and writing this affirmation for a period of time, then you have a block . . . or what I call a "counter-intention." You have a sabotaging thought buried somewhere and you must find it. This can be discovered and released easily by using the affirmation technique this book describes.

You will attract mates (actually you attract everyone in your life with your thoughts; this applies to attracting clients, business partners, and friends) who fit into your family patterns. After you understand and become cleared of those patterns you will automatically attract someone who is in harmony with your highest thoughts and then life will be easy. The best way to clear out old "neurotic" family patterns is through Rebirthing (a breathing process that clears your consciousness way back to birth) and through the processes in the Loving Relationships Training. Meanwhile, this book is a good way to get started.

PART ONE

The
Secrets

The
Secrets

When I was little, I got baptized, went to Sunday School, went to church, went to Bible camp, went to communion and even went to a church college for awhile. But there was one thing I could never figure out. Why was *my* father sick and on the verge of dying all the time? And why were all these people dying and what on earth *was* going on? I used to ask my minister why does He let people die or kill them? They never could answer me to my satisfaction. And when everyone said: "The Lord took him away," I could not and would not, reconcile *that*. It did not make any sense to me. I was left with the concept that God was something outside myself that was *in charge;* and if I didn't watch out, I might in fact, get the "Divine Meat Axe" any day! This concept not only made me very nervous, it did not work for me at all. And when my father actually died (when I was 15) that was it! I said, "If this is the result of God, I don't want any part of it." I ended up with insomnia for a whole year, among other painful things. I finally walked away from the church college I was attending in total confusion and total rebellion.

I ran away to the second biggest party school in the nation (according to *Playboy*) and I tried to have myself a good time. I did. I walked away from there married to an atheist. I was terrified of God, to put it mildly. Seven years later, and still in love with my husband, I ended up divorced, heartbroken, and going bald. Obviously this did not work either.

Wasn't there *some* answer? Where is the truth? What is the truth? I had to find it. I couldn't stand not knowing. I began a search that lasted 13 years. I literally traveled around the world looking for answers. When I found the answers and got clearer on what God is, I traveled even more to spread the word. Now, for 32 years I have been "on the road" and I'm willing to keep going.

I do know this: If you think it is God that kills people and destroys your relationships or punishes you and you blame "Him," you will find yourself in more trouble and your life will not work like it should. That concept does not work. It also doesn't work to think you can "leave God and forget about the whole thing." One day you will be forced to clear up your mind. One day you will be forced to see that you create your own universe with your mind, and even your own death by programming the whole thing. One day you will see that you have been given total free will and that God is the Great Affirmative that always says, "Yes," to your thoughts.

When I began to understand this, my relationships started working, and not before.

Clear Up Your Relationship With God

If you want your personal relationships to work, you must get clear on your relationship to God. When you are clear about who (or what) God is, then you have all the help you need for your relationships. If you are not clear about God, you may try to blame God for your troubles; you may even think that God punishes you or is out to get you.

God is the Source from which everything and everyone comes. If you don't have a good relationship with the Source, how can you have a good relationship with people? How can you love someone when you don't love the Source?

To have a good relationship with God, you must have some idea about God, and God has always been a difficult concept for people to understand. You may have felt confused about this, and you may have also felt guilty as you searched for the truth, especially if you have a strong childhood background in an orthodox religion. It may seem disloyal to your parents and religious teachers to consider breaking away from the creed they taught you as a child. However, such a search does not have to be destructive; it can enlarge upon your childhood conceptions and and strengthen them.

Maybe you have tried to run away from God, but how can you run away from your Source? You must maintain your oneness with God in order to be grounded in your own being. This is something that is up to you; God will not run after you if you try to leave. God lets you find yourself. Another way of putting this is to say that you are to work out your own salvation.

For more than two thousand years people in Western culture have feared God. In fact, we have hated God for putting us in what we thought was a closed universe where there was no escape from death. But the Age of Darkness is ending and the Age of True Enlightment is here. The truth need no longer be suppressed.

The truth is that God is the Great Affirmative that always says, "Yes," to your thoughts; God is *energy* added to your thoughts. If I say, "I am going to die when I am around seventy," God says, "Yes, whatever you say," and gives more energy to that thought. When we become clear that thought is creative, we can say, "I am giving up the thought that death is inevitable and I am *youthing!*"

As soon as we know that we have all of God's power available to us—as much as we can take—then everything changes. We can love God! We don't have to fear surrendering to God, because we know that God does not kill us.

The truth is that you are the Source, and part of the Source. In other words, you and the Source are inseparable. All your relationships are up to you; you can have them however you want them because God the Source pours energy into your thoughts and desires.

What is God?

GOD IS LOVE

What is God?

GOD IS ENERGY ADDED TO YOUR THOUGHTS

What is God?

GOD IS SIMPLY MORE OF YOU

Who are you? That is what you must determine. Your job is to learn who you are and how you are related to God. Begin now to see yourself healed and to see those around you healed. Love them as if you were God and they were God.

Get Enlightened

A long time ago, when I was married, I went for some private therapy and my husband and I went also for marriage counseling together. It never seemed to get us anywhere and I felt more upset because we had spent all that money and ended up divorced anyway. The trouble was, I wasn't enlightened and the counselors I went to weren't either. Now, I am very glad to say, times are changing. After I became enlightened, I became a counselor myself. I found marriage counseling to be the hardest thing I had ever had to do. I would see each spouse alone first for a half hour to an hour. Then I would see them together for an hour. It was grueling.

Bob and Joan were typical. She would blame him for their sex life not working and he would blame her. Then they would get together and blame each other to each other. They had no idea that their own thoughts from birth and childhood were getting in the way and that they were co-creating the mess with their subconscious thoughts, as well as the negative conscious ones they were yelling at each other. I had to stop them and give them a lecture on metaphysics. Finally, I told them it was too exhausting to work with them and I did not observe that they really wanted to change themselves. I added that I would only see them if they would agree to take the Loving Relationships Training first. It seemed unfair to have to give them the Training over and over, which took a long time on an individual basis and was costing them too much money. To my amazement, they agreed. After the Training, they only had to come to counseling once. It was very easy to work with them after they had both become enlightened.

Once *both parties* are enlightened, anything can be resolved. Until then it is often difficult, if not impossible.

This entire book is based on the definition of enlightenment given to me by Leonard Orr—it was the greatest gift I ever received:

ENLIGHTENMENT IS THE CERTAIN KNOWLEDGE OF THE ABSOLUTE TRUTH

The Absolute Truth is something that is true in all time and space, for everyone, equally, forever.

What is the Absolute Truth that leads to enlightenment?

THE ABSOLUTE TRUTH IS THAT
THOUGHT IS CREATIVE
or
THE THINKER IS CREATIVE WITH HIS THOUGHTS
(Any objection to the truth would be something you thought, which only goes to prove its validity.)

THE THINKER CREATES WITH HIS THOUGHTS
therefore
THOUGHTS PRODUCE RESULTS
therefore
YOUR NEGATIVE THOUGHTS PRODUCE NEGATIVE RESULTS FOR YOU
and
YOUR POSITIVE THOUGHTS PRODUCE POSITIVE RESULTS FOR YOU

God is Energy added to your thoughts, and always says, "Yes," to you. Therefore

WHAT YOU THINK ABOUT EXPANDS
and
WHAT YOU THINK ABOUT YOU GET MORE OF

Your thoughts produce results even though you are no longer consciously thinking them. If something terrible happens to you, you might have trouble taking responsibility for creating it if you are not in touch with the negative thought buried deep within you that originally created the situation. That is why it is so important to bring up and clear out those buried negative thoughts.

An example of a thought from birth that can mess up relationships is one which many women accepted the moment they were hung upside down and hit on the bottom by a male obstetrician: "Men hurt me."

Since the thinker is creative with his or her thoughts, this thought begins to produce results very early for a little girl. In kindergarten boys act out her beliefs by knocking her down or hitting her. She is teased by boys in grade school. Then in high school she starts dating and finds herself jilted because she still has the thought in her subconscious.

After a childhood and teenage of creating abuse from boys, she enters adulthood certain that men will hurt her. When a man comes along who seems to be nonthreatening she lays aside her anxieties and recovers long enough to fall in love and get married. When that doesn't work out and her husband runs off with her best friend, the old belief that "men hurt me" is reinforced and she resolves to have nothing further to do with men. All the time, the males in her life were simply acting out her lifelong subconscious belief. She herself, of course, was not even conscious of it.

Obviously, women act out men's thoughts in just the same way. A thought originating at birth for many men is that "Women want to suffocate (kill) me." Women may act this out by being too maternal and overprotective. Men usually interpret this as a sign that the women are trying to trap them. And so it goes. Thoughts create.

The way to rid outselves of these destructive subconscious thoughts is to do affirmations like this:

I forgive the doctor for the pain he caused me at birth.
I forgive my mother for the pain she caused me at birth.
I forgive myself for the pain I caused myself at birth.
Other men are not my obstetrician, or my father.
Other women are not my mother.

3

Use Affirmations

Betsy is typical of many clients I have had who have a very deep negative thought that nobody likes her or wants her. She was actually walking around with the thought in her subconscious "Nobody likes me, nobody wants me," and then she was wondering why her relationships would never work. Before she got enlightened she was helpless to do anything about this. A man would come along and try to love her. She could not compute this because it was against her basic belief about herself. She was actually putting out psychically to men a kind of command that went "Don't like me, don't want me." And so men responded to that telepathically and they didn't.

At first it was very hard for Betsy to believe that simply by changing her thoughts she could get a new result. I could empathize with her because I was once unable to believe it could be easy. She resisted doing the affirmation "Everybody likes me" because she said it was a lie. I explained to her that at first it will seem like a lie but she has to convince herself that it is not. I took her through it in stages. I had her write the following:

> Since I was the thinker that thought that nobody likes me
> and nobody wants me, I am also the thinker that can now
> think that people are starting to like me.

After she accepted the new thought, "People are starting to like me," she began to notice a few changes. People responded to her differently. Once some people responded to her differently she was able to convince herself more, and she was able to shift to the thought "People like me."

One has to re-program the mind as she did. It works. To help change a negative thought that you have had for a long time, take a deep breath, pull in the new thought on the inhale and let go of the old thought on the exhale.

An affirmation is a positive thought that you consciously choose to immerse in your consciousness to produce a certain desired result.

In other words, what you do is give your mind an idea on purpose. Your mind will certainly create whatever you want it to if you give it a chance. By repetition, you can feed your mind positive thoughts and achieve your desired goal. There are various ways to use affirmations.

Probably the simplest and most effective way that I have found is to write each affirmation ten or twenty times on a sheet of paper, leaving a space in the right-hand margin of the page for emotional "responses." As the affirmation is written on the left side of the page, you also jot down whatever thoughts, considerations, beliefs, fears, or emotions that may come into your mind on the right side of the page. Keep repeating the affirmation and observe how the responses on the right side change. A powerful affirmation will bring up all the negative thoughts and feelings stored deep in your consciousness and you will have the opportunity to discover what is standing between you and your goal. *The repetitive use of the affirmation will simultaneously make its impression on your mind and erase the old thought pattern, producing permanent desirable changes in your life!*

The truth is that thoughts produce results; and since realizations can very soon be discovered with this approach, the results are often startling.

Going back to the examples of negative thoughts in the last chapter, we can use the technique just explained to change a negative to a positive in the subconscious mind. Take the belief that "Men hurt me." Turning this around, you could say, "Men always want what is best for me." Then the exercise would go like this:

> Men always want what is best for me.
> *Like hell they do!*

> Men always want what is best for me.
> *No way.*

> Men always want what is best for me.
> *No. Feel like crying.*

> Men always want what is best for me.
> *Why should they?*

> Men always want what is best for me.
> *Dad ignored me.*

> Men always want what is best for me.
> *I don't deserve the best.*

> Men always want what is best for me.
> *I'm not that great.*

> Men always want what is best for me.
> *Ho ho ho.*

> Men always want what is best for me.
> *How could they?*

> Men always want what is best for me.
> *Can't imagine it.*

> Men always want what is best for me.
> *Tell me about it!*

> Men always want what is best for me.
> *You can't trust men.*

> Men always want what is best for me.
> *Could you trust a man?*

> Men always want what is best for me.
> *Oh, yeah?*

> Men always want what is best for me.
> *Best for them, you mean.*

Men always want what is best for me.
I know what men want . . .

Men always want what is best for me.
There might be one exception.

Men always want what is best for me.
Best for me?

Men always want what is best for me.
Is it possible?

Men always want what is best for me.
Could men care about me?

Men always want what is best for me.
Maybe they do.

Men always want what is best for me.
Can it be true?

Don't stop writing the affirmations and your reactions until no more negative responses come up. When you can write the affirmations and feel neutral, then your subconscious mind is being programmed with no interference.

As another example, remember the male who carried the negative thought that "Women want to suffocate (kill) me." This could be turned around to say, "Women always give me health and strength." Writing it over and over might produce responses like this:

Women always give me health and strength.
That's a laugh.

Women always give me health and strength.
They give me nothing but trouble.

Women always give me health and strength.
This is making me sad.

Women always give me health and strength.
Mother nags me.

Women always give me health and strength.
They don't even notice me.

Women always give me health and strength.
I can't trust them.

Women always give me health and strength.
Wish I could believe it.

Women always give me health and strength.
My throat aches; I want to cry.

Women always give me health and strength.
They won't even let me cry.

Women always give me health and strength.
I am afraid.

Women always give me health and strength.
Feeling confusion.

Women always give me health and strength.
Seems very risky.

Women always give me health and strength.
Might be possible.

Women always give me health and strength.
Wouldn't count on it.

Women always give me health and strength.
Maybe.

Women always give me health and strength.
Why shouldn't they?

These affirmation exercises will make you aware of what is already in your subconsciousness and will tell you how to make it work for you immediately. All you need is a willingness to look at yourself and a pen and paper or a typewriter—whatever is most comfortable for you.

After about a week of writing an affirmation, or when you have gotten in touch with most of the negative responses your mind makes to the affirmation, it is a good idea to stop using the response column and just keep writing the positive, affirming sentence. At this point you might want to switch to a tape cassette. I have found that it is just as effective for me to type affirmations; I am able to get ten written for each one I can do in longhand. Do what feels best for you.

Here is how to get the most out of the affirmations you do:

1. Work with one or more every day. The best times are

just before sleeping, before starting the day, or when you are feeling troubled.

2. Write each affirmation ten or twenty times.

3. Include your name in the affirmation. Say and write each affirmation to yourself in the first, second, and third persons as follows:

I, Sondra, forgive my mother for hurting me.

You, Sondra, forgive your mother for hurting you.

She, Sondra, forgives her mother for hurting her.

Writing in the second and third persons is often important, since your conditioning from others came to you in this manner.

4. Continue working with the affirmations daily until they become totally integrated into your consciousness. You will know this when your mind responds positively, and when you begin to experience the intended results. You will then experience mastery over your goals. You will be using your mind to serve you.

5. Record your affirmations on cassette tapes and play them back when you can. I very often play them while driving in the car on the freeway or when I go to bed. If I fall asleep while the earphone is still in my ear and the tape is going, the autosuggestion is still working as I sleep. (I am sure you are aware that I use affirmations in all areas of my life, for problems at work, problems with health, any problems at all. You can do the same.)

6. It is effective to look into the mirror and say the affirmations to yourself out loud. Keep saying them until you are able to see yourself with a relaxed, happy expression. Keep saying them until you eliminate all facial tension and grimaces.

7. Another method is to sit across from a partner, each of you in a straight back chair with your hands on your thighs and knees barely touching each other. Say the affirmation to your partner until you are comfortable doing it. Your partner can observe your body language carefully; if you squirm, fidget, or are unclear, you do not pass. He should not allow

you to go on to another one until you say it very clearly without contrary body reactions and upsets. When he does pass you, go on to the next affirmation. He can say them back to you, using the second person and your name. He should continue to say them to you until you can receive them well without embarrassment. This is harder than it sounds.

Another alternative at any time, of course, is to say them to yourself. You may not always feel like writing. However, writing is more powerful because more of the senses are involved.

So as you begin reading now, note which affirmations have the greatest emotional reaction or "charge" for you and mark them as you go. Try to have a good time discovering the secrets to your own consciousness. If you ever get to a point where you begin to feel upset, shaky, or afraid about something negative you learn about yourself, don't panic. Keep on writing the applicable affirmation over and over until your mind takes on the new thought. As it does, the negativity will be erased and you will feel lighter and better. Remember: It is just as easy to think positively as negatively. In fact it is easier. Negative thinking actually takes more effort.

Don't settle for so little in your life! You deserve a lot!

Beginning Affirmation Exercises

1. I, _____, was born with a limitless capacity for loving and fulfilling relationships.

2. I, _____, have a basic trust that my affirmations will work and my efforts will be rewarded.

3. I, _____, am willing to move through my barriers of ignorance, fear, and anger, so that my perfect being can express itself in all my relationships.

4. Loving relationships are a key element in my state of general health and well-being.

5. Every negative thought automatically triggers my creative mind to think of three desirable positive thoughts.

For more on affirmations, see Appendix B, page 156.

Get Rebirthed Frequently

In every single Rebirth I have ever done, I learned something new about the effects of the birth trauma on the individual's relationships in later life. I was astonished. This information was so valuable that I put it all together in my head and the results have become an integral part of the Loving Relationships Training.

One of the more drastic cases I had was a fellow named John. He was a breech baby. When he came out "butt first," his mother bled a lot and almost died. His conclusion, established at birth, was this: "In order to survive I have to hurt someone, especially a woman." He had no memory of that decision, of course, but when he came to me he was ready to kill himself and felt outright suicidal. His complaint was that he had some kind of syndrome in which he kept hurting people, especially women. He said he had become a homosexual. (I am sure you can see the connection: When he was "inside a woman" she might die and this terrified him.) He had no recollection of his birth and he felt like Rebirthing would be the last thing he would try before he did himself in.

I remember that his Rebirth was long and deep and that he had a continuous flood of pictures and memories, including coming out breech, the blood and his mother's near-death.

Once all these "connections" were made and I was able to design appropriate affirmations for him, he saw there was hope to escape from this syndrome and he chose to live.

What does your birth experience have to do with your relationships? More than you ever dreamed! All of the following emotional responses are closely related to your birth:
1. Fear of entrapment in a relationship
2. Womb-like dependency on a mate
3. Fear of pleasure
4. Separation anxiety
5. Fear of letting go with people
6. Fear of receiving love; distrust of people
7. Sexual problems
8. Poor self-image; feeling less than another
9. Feeling like you are dying when a partner leaves you
10. Suppressed anger and rage
    and more!

Our research has shown that the roots of these common problems go right back to the womb and the first five minutes of life. Before Rebirthing was discovered, it was very hard to get down to the personal laws formed at birth that govern our lives. I like to say that this will likely be the first generation of people whose relationships really work because they are dealing with the birth-death cycle.

Rebirthing not only cures permanently the fears that ruin relationships, but it also heals you in every way. As you breathe out negative mental mass, retained from birth, you feel healthier, more alive, more beautiful, and more lovable. You naturally begin to attract fabulous people into your life with whom it is easy to have a loving, exciting relationship.

Some examples of the decisions I made at birth that have always affected my relationships with men were these:
1. I can't love this. It hurts. Life hurts.
2. I can't trust men if this is what they are going to do to me.

3. Men can't be depended upon when I need them.
4. This is too much. I hate you. Stay out of my life.

With thoughts like these it is a wonder I ever allowed any man to get close to me. The truth is that at the beginning of a relationship thoughts like this tend to be suppressed. But once love begins to flow, the thoughts start to surface. (This is because love brings up anything unlike itself.) Those subconscious thoughts would begin to rear their ugly heads and produce results, even though I was no longer consciously thinking them. When the thoughts came up enough, the relationship would blast apart. (This usually happens when both partners' patterns are surfacing at the same time.)

Since I had buried thoughts from birth like "Men aren't there for me" and "Stay out of my life," having a man stay with me was not compatible with my programming. Therefore I would have to create his leaving to support my pattern; it is like supporting a drug or alcohol habit. The men, even if they loved me very, very much, would run up against my pattern and find they had to give me what I expected—which was NOT to be there. So if they tried to stay, I would set them up to leave.

Before I became enlightened, I did not know I had these buried thoughts. Since I still believed in blame, it was next to impossible to recognize the thoughts as my own, and my relationships always ended up the same. It has taken the energy of the LRT, the energy of Rebirthing, and the energy of God and affirmations to blast these out of me.

A *personal law* (which we now call a *personal lie*) is your most negative thought about yourself, usually formed at birth. Now you can see how important it is to become aware of your own personal laws if you want to have good relationships. You can follow through by thoroughly studying Rebirthing in the Appendix.

5

Love Yourself

I once knew a very beautiful woman who had everything, it seemed. But she was always messing up her life and she once lost everything, including most of her wealth. She was a twin and she had been born first and healthy. Her sister who had come out second had always been sick and unsuccessful in life. My client hated herself because she thought she ruined her sister's life by coming out first. She ended up thinking "I am a bad person." So, even though she was ravishingly beautiful, men stayed away from her because she did not like herself; and she did not treat herself well at all because she thought she should punish herself. (People treat you the way you treat yourself.)

Another woman hated herself because she could not be the baby that had died before she was born. She felt her parents really wanted *that* baby instead and they had her to "make up for the loss." She felt she could never be who they wanted and she hated herself. She too was a beautiful woman but it did not matter because she would always attract men who would beat her up in one form or another. She felt guilty that she could not be who her parents wanted and she made sure to punish herself.

I have had many clients who hated themselves because they

did not come out as the sex their parents wanted. And the list goes on and on. People hate themselves for a million different things. People who hate themselves often get fat and then they hate themselves more. Or they conjure up some other way to prove how bad they are.

It is very hard for them to get out of self-hate unless they are aware of the strong negative thoughts they may have formed about themselves way back at birth or even in the womb.

Self-hate makes one ugly. Every person I have seen who gave up their self-hate and who forgave everything became more and more beautiful right before my eyes.

Here is a metaphysical law:

PEOPLE TREAT YOU
THE WAY YOU TREAT YOURSELF

Jesus said, "Love thy neighbor as *thyself.*"

One definition of love is ultimate self-approval. If you love yourself, you will automatically give others the opportunity to love you. If you hate yourself, you will not allow others to love you. If your self-esteem is low and someone loves and accepts you, you will reject them, try to change them, or think they are lying.

When you blame the world for lacking love, you are creating still more negative mental mass, which makes things worse for you.

One excellent definition of love is this: ""Love is an all-existing substance noticed mostly in the absence of negative thought" (Kyle Os). Some people taking the Training feel real love for the first time because they become stripped of the negativity that kept them from noticing the love in the first place. Some of this negativity is buried, and you may not know you have it. Often it takes the energy of a large group to push it out of you.

Sometimes people tell me, "My life doesn't work because I don't have the right mate." That philosophy will never work. You must *become* the right person rather than looking for the right person. In order to attract the cream of the crop you must become the cream of the crop. To become the person you would want for a mate, we have devised processes in the Training to raise your self-esteem.

Here are some other ways to increase your self-love:

1. Acknowledge and praise yourself verbally to yourself.
2. Approve of all your own actions; learn from them.
3. Have confidence in your ability.
4. Give yourself pleasure without guilt.
5. Love your body and admire your beauty.
6. Give yourself what you want; feel that you deserve it.
7. Let yourself win — in life and in relationships.
8. Allow others in to love you.
9. Follow your own intuition.
10. See your own perfection.
11. Let yourself be rich; give up poverty.
12. Reward yourself; never punish yourself.
13. Trust yourself.
14. Nourish yourself.
15. Let yourself enjoy sex and affection.
16. Turn all your negative thoughts about yourself into affirmations.

P.S. High self-esteem is not being egotistical; "Egotism is trying to prove you're OK after you've fallen into hating yourself." (Marshall Summers).

6

Love Your Body
and
Handle the Unconscious
Death Urge

I have also learned in Rebirthing that people often start hating their bodies right at birth. I have had clients who made the decision "My body causes me pain," as they were being born and experiencing trauma. Then, because they have had that thought, they did in fact create bodies that were filled with pain for most of their lives. Eventually it became just "too much" and they even wanted to die in order to be free. And since much of the pain from the birth trauma is stored in the body and, in some cases, is felt constantly, it is no wonder that our ancestors left their bodies. It was too painful to stay in them after years of accumulating negative mental mass.

It *is* hard to love your body when it hurts. That is, of course, when you need to love it the most because it is trying to teach you something.

After my father died, I had a pain in my body that migrated around to different places. I actually had this pain for ten years, and I tried to heal it with psychiatrists, regular physicians, physical therapists, and hypnotists, with a few "medicine men" thrown in. Nothing worked. The more I had it, the more I hated it; the more I hated my body, the less I wanted to live. I got myself into a vicious circle. It wasn't until I got to

Rebirthing and breathed out my pain and death urge permanently that it went away. It went away totally after three Rebirths.

Now that I am actually living in a body free of tension
and pain, my body is a pleasurable place to be. It makes me
want to live because I always feel good. It makes me want
to extend life. It makes me easier to be around. By the way,
just sleeping next to someone who has cleared out the bulk
of the birth trauma and death urge is a whole and new wonderful experience. There is, in fact, a new vibration to your cells
(they "sing") once you clear out that negative mental mass.

If you don't love your body, you don't love yourself. And if
you don't love yourself, how can you expect someone else to
love you or your body?

How can you love your body when you think it is unattrac-
tive and not the way you want it to be? You must recognize
that your body seems ugly to you because you have ugly
thoughts about it. You can change your body by changing your
thoughts.

First, acknowledge your body for obeying your instructions. It deserves to be loved for doing just what you tell
it to do. Remember, you chose it, so you can't blame your
parents either. Your body is your perfect mirror of yourself.
You can clear your body as you clear your mind. It is never
too late. When we work on the mind in the Training, we
see people become beautiful right before our eyes. When
your thoughts about yourself and life become beautiful, you
become beautiful.

How often has your physical pain or illness made you
grumpy and hard to live with? How often have your physical
ailments affected your relationships? Conversely, how often
have the ailments been the result of a relationship that you
are not handling?

A very effective way of creating good health and a beautiful body for yourself is to search out all the negatives about

your body that you have buried and transform them into affirmations.

Another incredibly successful process for getting in touch with your body is Rolfing. Rolfing is a system that could be described as deep body work combined with very high consciousness. To me, Rolfers are like enlightened sculptors of the body who understand that the body is a highly plastic instrument that can be molded. Along with Rebirthing, Rolfing helps to make your body flexible, softer, more aligned with gravity, and much more beautiful and alluring.

There is just no excuse to stay ugly anymore. You can no longer blame your looks for your troubles or for not having lovers. Now that we can change our looks and our form from within, there are no more excuses for not having great relationships. We must ask ourselves if we want reasons or results. We must give up the habit of misery and self-pity. We can help ourselves.

Need I mention how loving your own body will affect your sex life? Obviously if you love your body totally you will allow it to have pleasure. *In sex, you will only let yourself receive as much as you are willing to give yourself.* So . . . sex is up to you!

7

Handle Anger and
Suppressed Negativity

I have had many clients who grew up in families where there were constant fights raging. Often these families loved each other underneath it all, but they had no idea how to express love. They did know how to express anger. The children of these families ended up with the idea that love *was* anger. In other words, they did not feel they were being loved unless they were being yelled at. They actually had it wired up so that anger was love. In their relationships they would create situations to make their partners really angry so they would be yelled at. They actually liked being yelled at; however, nothing ever got resolved. My work with them, Rebirthing and the LRT, helped them to rewire anger and love.

At the other extreme, I have had many clients in Rebirthing who thought that anger was an absolute no-no. It had been forbidden totally in their families. Usually people in their family stuffed the anger and never expressed it. These people grew up never expressing anger themselves and they would set up a situation where others got angry around them (and for them to ease the psychic tension) or they would end up with a condition called "covert hostility"—they never even knew when they were angry. I tended more toward this extreme myself; and it was a long time before I found out that not only are all emotions OK, expressing them is OK. But most of all I learned that there are safe and appropriate ways to handle anger that do not hurt a relationship.

It is important to recognize that

LOVE BRINGS UP ANYTHING UNLIKE ITSELF

When we receive a lot of love from someone, the stuff unlike love will come out of us in the form of anger, sadness, fear, pain, upset, and all other suppressed negativity. Our partners are healing us by pushing this negativity out of us.

LOVE ALWAYS HEALS . . . IF YOU LET IT

Often it is very frightening to be in a wonderful new relationship and suddenly have ugly negative feelings come to the surface. However, when you understand that love brings up anything unlike itself you will be able to see it as an opportunity for healing.

The first thing that might come up is suppressed anger. In *est* and in the *Course in Miracles* we learn: "You are never upset for the reason you think." Therefore don't blame your partners and become angry with them. What they did probably stirred up in you the memory of something similar for which you have not forgiven someone.

I am not saying you should not express your anger. Just don't project it onto someone else. Anger is always an opportunity to know yourself better. Here are some suggestions for handling your anger in appropriate ways:

1. Go out for a drive and scream in the car, or go scream in the shower. Scream nice things to yourself after you get the initial rage out.

2. Get Rebirthed and breathe out the anger. (Inhale love and exhale anger.)

3. Get Rolfed to release suppressed anger from your body. Breathe well during the Rolfing.

4. Write out angry feelings in the form of a letter you can later tear up.

5. Get encounter bats or boffing sticks, which are padded, and hit a chair or bat each other. (These are designed to be harmless.) Be sure to breathe.

6. Do forgiveness processes.

7. Lie on a bed with legs and knees *straight.* Keeping *knees locked,* do the scissors kick, pounding your heels into the bed. Keep breathing!

8. Affirm that you are ready to forgive everyone in your past and present. Ask for help; tell God you are ready to totally forgive.

9. Know that anger in someone else is an appeal for help and healing. *Don't match energies.* Just keep breathing and, after they have finished, ask, "How can I support you?"

My friend Phil Laut and I were corresponding some years ago about the subject of anger. We want to understand it better and to find better ways to handle it with our students and Rebirthees. Here is an excerpt from one of his letters:

> Anger usually results in the desire to manipulate or in the feeling of rejection. Failing to get what he wants, the angry person endeavors to manipulate others to get his way. Not asking for what you want is a subtle way to manipulate people. (If I ask you for milk when I really want Scotch, then I can "make you wrong" when you bring me milk. If you are clever enough to read my mind and bring Scotch, then I can make you wrong for not bringing what I asked for.)
>
> There are several ways to let go of anger. One is to notice that your body is safe. Another is to tell the truth to yourself if you are wanting love. There is nothing wrong with wanting love, except if you don't tell the truth to yourself about it, it can keep you angry forever.

In another letter, my friend Bill Chappelle wrote some words about blame:

> The problem is that some people confuse self-sufficiency with rebellion against or rejection of someone else. This problem begins by first seeing the other person as the

cause in your life, then giving them your power, then blaming them if things do not work out for you. So if a person loves himself and is doing exactly what he wants to do, you may tend to blame him if you are not doing exactly what you want to do. The emotion that follows is often anger or helplessness. It may be followed by the decision to quit, get out, start over, or find another person to depend on and blame for what is ultimately your own insecurity.

The Course in Miracles Explanation by Kenneth Wapnich (a booklet published by the Foundation for Inner Peace) says this:

Hate and anger are but attempts to project guilt from within ourselves onto another person. Anger, according to the Course, always involves such projection, no matter how justified it appears to be. The external situation is never a sufficient explanation for our hostile reactions. Only the ego values anger. The more we attack, the guiltier we become, and the greater our need to project and be attacking again.

Remember that

BLAME IS ALWAYS OFF THE TRACK

Whenever you feel like blaming your mate or another, STOP. Take a look to see what the response that makes you feel like blaming says about you and how you might have created that response.

You will learn a lot about yourself and you will save your relationship every time you communicate your part in creating the result that was obtained.

8

Tell the
Complete Truth
Faster

Because children are very psychic and can often read people's minds, and even at times see their auras, they might blurt out something that not only seems weird to a parent, but something that is hard on the nerves as well as the hearing, like "Mommie, I saw purple around Uncle Harry's head!" or "Uncle Bill really hates Aunt Sarah and wishes she'd die." About this time a mother might, in fact, punish the child for saying such ridiculous things. After that a child might decide that if he tells the truth he will be punished. Then he tends to grow up either telling lies in order to save his face or avoid telling what he sees and feels. Probably, he will "lose" or suppress his ability to see auras and truth.

I have found that it is very hard to keep a relationship clean when the truth is suppressed. I have found that it is very hard to clean up a relationship when people are afraid to tell the truth.

One has to begin by using affirmations like these:

"It is now safe for me to tell the truth."
"I can tell my true feelings safely."
"People love it when I tell the truth."
"Telling the truth always heals."

Just today, a graduate who was talking to me long distance

on the phone said that he was so happy; his relationship was finally working since he had practiced the training and especially since they had been telling the truth about what they felt. "It is so simple," he added.

One day, co-trainer Bobby Birdsall, said to me, "Let's make an agreement to have more fun per hour and to tell the complete truth faster."

"Fabulous," I said. "I like that so much that I'd like to make it the motto of the Loving Relationships Training."

Werner Erhard of *est* once said, "What you can't communicate runs you." I certainly agree. People are telepathic, whether you like it or not, so don't try to fool anybody for a second. The body never lies. Stewart Emery of Actualizations says that communication is 40 percent verbal and 60 percent nonverbal. This means that you are easy to read if you are suppressing something. It is also very painful and harmful to your body.

People are afraid to tell each other some things because they think they might hurt the other person or themselves. Well, it hurts you both much more if you fail to communicate whatever it is. First of all, your body will be in pain if you are withholding communication; second, the other person will become confused; and third, the relationship will get crazy. The truth will come out eventually anyway, and by then the mistrust and anger may be so great that the whole relationship will blow up.

Begin with this thought: *It is safe to tell the truth, and the more I tell the truth about my feelings the better I will feel and the better others will feel.*

If you tell a lie about something, you may have to tell another lie to cover up the first one. Eventually you will have a big mess on your hands and your relationships will never work.

THE TRUTH WORKS. THE TRUTH HEALS.

Tell it as fast as you can. Tell what the truth is for you right now. People will love you for it. You will feel good for doing it. Tell how you *feel!*

9

Clear Up the Ten Patterns

A man named Herb once told me that after his divorce he had dated many women and he had noticed that they were all just like his ex-wife. He said they could have all been right out of the same mold. They were all destructive to his life and yet he could not stop himself from attracting this type of woman. He felt he might as well have been addicted to alcohol or drugs, as he recognized this syndrome as being like an addiction. He was, however, smart enough to not marry any of these women or he probably would have been divorced over and over again.

After he learned about ten patterns in the LRT, he was amazed at how simple it all was. Each woman was like the stepfather he hated. Once he was able to forgive his stepfather, he stopped attracting that kind of woman.

A woman in one training jumped up in this section of the training and started screaming, ''My God, I have been marrying my nanny.'' She had been raised by a cranky English nanny and all the men she married were just like her. She was on her third husband.

Once you get yourself out of the ''patterns'' life is totally different. Until then, there is a tendency to go through an endless stream of parental substitutes for mates.

Have you ever found yourself doing the same old thing in every new relationship, even though you hoped things would be different when you got a "new" partner? If so, you are probably stuck in a "pattern."

A pattern is a repetitive unconscious behavior. This is descriptive of the tendencies I have seen in relationships — at least in the old neurotic relationships of the past. Clearing out these patterns is imperative to having good relationships. Here are ten patterns I have identified that continue to show up in relationships. I'm sure there are more; however, these seem to be the most common.

Pattern 1. Since you established your first relationship with your parents, you tend to recreate their *personalities* as closely as possible in your other relationships.

Pattern 2. You will tend to recreate the *kind of relationships* you had with your parents in your other relationships.

Pattern 3. You will tend to copy the relationships your parents had *with each other.*

Pattern 4. Since most of us are used to a heavy dose of parental disapproval, we will tend to create upsets that will make our partner disapprove of us.

Pattern 5. You will tend to get even with your parents by using your mate or another. If your mate won't allow this, you might use your children.

Pattern 6. Most people subconsciously want to remain helpless children all of their lives. A conflict will occur when each wants to be a child and each wants the other to be his or her parent.

Pattern 7. Since most people are used to the struggle they had with their parents, having a totally successful, easy, smooth relationship is often too unfamiliar to tolerate, and too threatening.

Pattern 8. Suppressed incest always stands in the way of sexual affection. The point at which you could not acknowledge sexual feelings for your parents (or they for you) is the point where your sexuality became inhibited.

Pattern 9.   Because of self-hate and guilt there is the tendency to "beat yourself up" by using one of the following: Your body/your sex life/your career/your mate/your finances/your car.

a.   In other words, there is a tendency to mess up one or all of these relationships to punish yourself for something.

b.   The guilt and self-hate can go all the way back to thinking you separated yourself from God by taking on a body; thinking that you are bad because you caused your mother pain at birth. It is very deep.

c.   It, of course, can be due to anything else that you did that was a "wrongdoing" in your own eyes. Children often blame themselves for their parents' divorces or deaths, for example.

d.   Another way of "beating yourself up" for these things is not to let yourself have what you really deserve. Not receiving your good. A most common way is to ruin your body somehow with obesity, pain, or disease.

e.   This all results in a thought: I hate myself; I am a bad person. Then you will attract someone that will prove it.

Pattern 10.   You will attract someone who fits your patterns. That is, if you have a pattern that says "Men leave me," you will tend to attract a man who has a pattern of leaving.

You will find much greater contentment if you clear out your patterns. Then, instead of attracting someone who fits your patterns, you can attract someone in harmony with your highest spiritual thoughts.

10

Clean Up Old Relationships

It took me years to clean up my relationship with my ex-husband. The day we parted we were still so much in love and so shocked that we were separating that we could hardly speak. Neither of us understood it at all. Whenever we tried to get together it was so emotional that we just cried. Once we met in Scottsdale a year after we were divorced. He had been in Brazil. I had been a nurse in the Air Force. He ordered champagne, roses, and a gourmet meal. We took one look at each other and we both started to sob. We could not speak or eat.

A year after that we tried it again. I was determined to clear it up. We met in Atlanta and got a motel room. He said to me, "You must be angry at me for the way I treated you, so why don't you just beat me up a little bit?" We had never laid a hand on each other all the time we were married and I guess he thought maybe we should have. When he laid himself down at my feet, literally, I came unglued. I could not move. Things did not work much better that year.

In my determination to heal that relationship, I began to study relationships intently. After a few years of Rebirthing and after I had just begun to put together a seminar or two, it came to me how obviously easy it would be to clean it up. Now that I was enlightened, it was in fact simple. Perhaps I can save you a few years of trying to figure it out. The simple answer in this chapter worked for me. Every graduate that has used it found it to work. My only regret is that it took me so long to figure out.

It is very important to go back through your past and clean up all your old relationships. Every unresolved relationship from the past drains off a little or a lot of your vital energy. Resolving old hurts releases that energy to increase your power and zest in the present.

The place to start cleaning up old relationships is with your parents, because

ANYTHING UNRESOLVED WITH YOUR PARENTS WILL COME UP IN YOUR RELATIONSHIPS

Generally the things our partners do that upset us are things we have not forgiven our parents for doing. When you have totally forgiven your parents for whatever is unresolved, either your partner will stop doing the upsetting thing or you will find another partner without that problem. It is likely that, without knowing it, your partner was trying to heal you by acting out your parents' behavior for you.

LOVE TAKES YOUR NEGATIVE UPON ITSELF SO THAT YOU CAN SEE IT MORE CLEARLY

This means that your mate makes an unconscious attempt to heal you by acting out roles and negatives of your past so that you can process that aspect out of your consciousness. Most of us don't know that is what is happening, so we begin to blame our mates. All the while, we are really angry at our mother or father or some parental substitute of the past.

Eventually we must clean up all the relationships of the past that are not completely resolved. How can you know if the relationship is cleaned up? Consider the past and present relatives, friends, and lovers in your life. If you have any feelings for them other than unconditional love when you think of their name, then those relationships are not cleaned up.

11

Clean Up Relationships Daily

I remember one couple (and many others) who had the following pattern: Dave would be angry with Janet for something but he would not tell her. He would decide maybe he shouldn't tell her and then he would pretend to "get over it." But he would be seething inside. Janet had the exact same tendency. She would never tell Dave what made her angry with him. They would both "stuff it." Then the pressure would build and build and finally they would have a knock-down drag-out fight and scream out all the things they had stored up. This was "dumping" on the highest order. They were always fighting about things that happened two months ago, sometimes even a year ago. They were never in present time and one or the other would always deny that they said or did that thing two months ago. Then they would get in a fight about a fight. It was a mess.

After the training they literally started *all over*. They confessed to me that they had both been suicidal before the Training because they could not seem to get themselves out of this syndrome. They made a simple agreement afterwards to clean up their relationship every night or on the spot if possible, but at least every night. They both stuck to this agreement and it worked. Besides, they found out that they were not really upset with each other for the reasons they thought and there was not much to fight about anymore. But when something did come up, they would express it on the same day, and start each new day fresh as though they had a "new" relationship.

It is a good policy to have an agreement in your present relationship that you will clean it up at least every night. It is better to clean up things on the spot, but sometimes that is not always appropriate. But if you want a light, joyful relationship, don't wait another day to communicate something.

Each night you can simply say to your roommate, lover, or spouse, "Is there anything you need to communicate to me before we go to sleep?" If you do this, then nothing builds up and each new day starts well. Eventually this process will become integrated into your life as a good habit and you won't even need to ask the questions to remind each other.

After you have been Rebirthed and Rolfed you will hunger to communicate these things the same day; waiting any longer will be too uncomfortable in your body because you will be extra sensitive to all vibrations.

The amount of love that flows between the two of you is often controlled by the quantity and quality of your communications. After you have cleaned up the day's withheld communications, complete the process by acknowledging yourself and your partner for successes. Then you can drop off to sleep in a happy state of mind, or have sex without a lot of "psychic garbage" between you.

12

Find the Highest
Spiritual Thought

Many couples I have worked with argue because they each get stuck on their "position." He thinks for sure he is right and she thinks for sure she is right. Neither will budge from their position and they continue to fight. This could go on for years and years. I assure you, there *is* another way to play the game and it is also exciting.

Marvin and Thelma were fighting about whether or not they should move. Thelma said they had outgrown the house and there was not enough room anymore for their things. She felt crowded and depressed; and besides the house was always damp and musty because of the way it was located. This problem had gotten worse over the years and there seemed to be no way to get rid of the dampness. Marvin said they could never get another house for that amount of money and they could not afford anything else. They fought about this continually. They went 'round and 'round and 'round and there was never a resolution. I told them it was time to *go for solution* and that there was a higher spiritual thought. That thought was that they could *both* win. It had never occurred to them, for some reason that they could both win.

I asked them to try seeing things newly. I asked them to entertain the thought that they *could* find a house that was spacious, dry and warm and at a price that was just as reasonable. Or they could surrender to the thought that they could literally get rid of some of the things they had and find some way to clear up the dampness. Both thoughts were positive as opposed to the two negative positions that they had had earlier. The first step was that at least they each got off their negative positions. The next step was to find the highest thought that would enable them to each get what they wanted. They chose to move. Because Marvin surrendered to a higher thought than the one he had (he went from "It is impossible" to "It might be possible") they did in fact find a new house at a reasonable price.

It was in fact only a little bit more, but because there were more rooms in it, Thelma was able to start her own little mail order business at home and they soon had more money plus a new house.

There is always another way where both of you can win.

Never allow yourself to stay stuck in any position. Like Bobby and me, always be willing to discover and accept a higher spiritual thought. You can always feel and know which is the highest thought by listening to your body. The highest thought is always the one that is most positive, the least limiting, and the most truthful and the most productive. It "feels" the best in your body. This game prevents all power struggles and fights. It has been adopted by trainers, and certified Rebirthers play it naturally. People learn to play it in the Training and are always developing their skill at it.

When each person is always willing to surrender to the highest spiritual thought, this does not imply that someone gives power away to another. With a couple, sometimes one may have the higher spiritual thought, sometimes the other partner will have it. If my partner has it, I leave my position and rise to the level of the higher thought. If I have the higher thought, my partner does the same.

In business meetings or other group situations, we evolve the highest thought. When the highest thought has been presented and everyone recognizes it, then people stop being "stuck" and rise to the new level. Everyone is relieved and happy no matter who came up with the thought. When confusion arises as to which is the highest thought, we go apart and meditate rather than fight it out.

Always look at your life to see what results you are creating and attracting. Then consider what thoughts you must have had to produce these results. A most important time to remember this is when your mate is reacting to you in some way that you don't like. Look at yourself and see why you might be creating that kind of behavior from your mate and what part of your subconscious desired that reaction. You must also take responsibility for attracting the kind of person into your life who demonstrates that behavior.

Work on your own to upgrade the level of your thoughts, and ask your partner to do the same. You will be amazed at the results.

13

Give Up Guilt

Once Bobby and I were shocked to find ourselves in a pattern of losing things. We each had lost gold jewelry, money, and some very good clothes. We set our minds to figure this out before it got worse. We stopped in New York to talk it over with our friend, Bob Mandell. We did some simple processes on ourselves, with Bob's help, just like we do in the LRT.

We finally realized that we were suffering from plain old guilt because we were having it too good and we were having too much fun. (People in our culture often get the idea that pleasure is bad and even that "good is bad." You don't dare have it "too good," whatever that is.) Compared to most people we were just having too much fun and so we had to balance it out a little by getting rid of some things in order to not feel guilty. We then all decided that we had to get rid of guilt instead of getting rid of "things." We came up with the joke of giving up guilt for Lent. Bobby said, "Yeah, let's kill guilt."

Shortly after that we left on our way to Denver. On the way to Kennedy airport, we got ourselves behind a funeral procession. Bobby looked at me and quipped, "It is the death of guilt." I laughed and we got on the plane. In Denver we got off the plane and lo and behold, three graduates who picked us up came in an old hearse! We took guilt to the grave and the problem cleared up.

Guilt very often "runs" or controls relationships. This includes your relationship with money! Guilt is a symptom (much in the same way that fever is a symptom) that something is out of kilter in your relationship with the universe. If you are clear that you are a perfect manifestation of the Source, then guilt makes no sense. So guilt arises when we let ourselves forget our own divinity. Christians have identified sin as separation from God. The *Course in Miracles* says, "The continuing decision to remain separated is the only possible reason for continuing guilt feelings."

Many people go along letting their relationships work well and giving themselves a lot of pleasure until they suddenly reach their pleasure tolerance. This is an artificial barrier they have set up for themselves which is controlled by guilt. The minute they start feeling guilty for having a wonderful relationship or for having an abundance of money they will begin messing it up.

You have to work out guilt in order to believe you deserve a good relationship. You have to work out guilt to allow yourself to have all the pleasure that comes along with a perfect relationship. And you have to work out guilt to handle money successfully.

You can start by forgiving yourself for any failures or transgressions you think you have had. Meditate on the thought *I am innocent. My innocence brings peace, love, and abundance to me.*

RETURN TO INNOCENCE by Phil Laut

Innocence is a state of oneness with yourself; it is a state of *now knowing*. This means that your perception of yourself is free of past knowledge or conditioning; it leaves you free to function in present time.

Guilt is the fear reaction to what you may perceive as an unsafe universe. Guilt is the tendency to beat the universe to the punch and punish yourself before something bigger and stronger can punish you. Guilt is its own punishment. If you feel guilty, you have already punished yourself enough. More punishment will not make you feel any better.

Forgiveness is the path of the return to innocence — the return to the natural human state of unconditional love, satisfaction, peace and power. Forgiveness is letting go of all attachment to thoughts of revenge or retribution. Forgiveness is emotional disarmament.

Forgiveness is not logical in the standard sense of logic. Forgiveness is very simple. If you feel guilty about something, that is all the information you need to know that forgiveness is lacking. Forgiveness has nothing to do with anyone but you. When you forgive someone, you may notice that they feel better about you, but that is not the point. Forgiveness is so that *you* can feel better about yourself. So, just as guilt is its own punishmnent, forgiveness is its own reward.

Jesus said, when asked how many times should someone forgive, "Seventy times seven." An effective way to practice this idea is to write forgiveness affirmations seventy times per day for a week. Guilt is all you have to lose by doing this.

Basic Forgiveness Affirmations

1. I forgive myself for hurting others.
2. I forgive others for hurting me.
3. I forgive myself for letting others hurt me.
4. I forgive others for letting me hurt them.

Other Forgiveness Affirmations

5. I forgive myself for accepting food when I wanted love.
6. I forgive myself for pretending to be right when I wanted love.
7. I forgive the doctor for forcing me to breathe at birth.
8. I forgive myself for forcing the doctor to get me to breathe at birth.
9. I forgive myself for struggling in life.

10. I am innocent, I am a Child of God. All my desires are holy and they always have been.

Rima

I remember the night that I became REALLY fascinated with Rima. I had certified her months before in Texas and she deserved it then. But it was not until August 1980 at the Rebirther's Jubilee in Sun Valley, Idaho, that I really got into adoration of her. We were celebrating Mallie and Bob's marriage. I was very happy. Rima was ecstatic. She was about seven months pregnant. I looked at her at the end of the table glowing most of the night. She looked exotically beautiful. Her physical beauty was one thing. Her spiritual beauty was the main thing. Her presence was amazing to me. Her own presence blew me away, let alone the being inside of her. I was rather stunned. A very deep rush of love occurred inside me.

Was this the woman who last year was someone else? She had not been ready then and I could not sign her Rebirther's paper, which was very hard on me. It was I who was the last to sign. It hurt me, but I had to be tough on her. It seemed to me that the whole State of Texas—and Rebirthing—were on the line. I felt there was one important piece of her birth trauma that was left. Six months later when I saw her in Texas, it was lifting. She looked different. A new pregnancy was healing her and she was smart enough to know that. I remember the moment she surrendered to me completely and "got off it," as we say in Rebirther's jargon. She told the group in Texas that she completely understood my hesitancy six months before in Colorado and she told everyone how it had served her. I felt change in my body regarding her. There was tremendous relief, a tremendous love. I told her I would certify her in front of the others when we met in Santa Barbara, but to me that was her day, that was her certification day then and there in Texas. To me it is always like a rite of passage, and I was once again deeply moved.

We began to celebrate on a long drive to Abby's ranch (near LBJ's). We celebrated all day. In the late afternoon Abby, the hostess, went into a complete spontaneous rebirth and fell on the floor in front of me. It was one of the most complex rebirths I have ever had to do. Rima was perfect. She felt it from the other room and came in to assist me at the perfect moment. Her time was perfect. Her approach was perfect. Everything about her was perfect and I appreciated her help very much.

Rima drove when we went back to Austin. Rima and Lucy and I were in the front seat. Rima's husband, Steve, was in the back seat with the new Rebirthee, Abby, who was still integrating it all. There was a lot of emotion and intensity in the car—to put it mildly. I asked Rima if it was bothering her to drive. She glanced at me with a twinkle in her eyes and quipped, "I am a Certified Chauffeur" in her darling Texas accent. We were both delighted at the multiple meanings of that statement. Every good rebirther knows how to rebirth someone while driving.

Soon I had the first occasion to have her share leadership of a Loving Relationships Training with me. It was the first Texas LRT. Since she was new as a trainer, I explained to her that at her first training she was expected to sit silently in the front of the room with me and not to say a word. Her assignment was to learn mastery of handling and channeling the immense energy in the room (which is unique compared to any other training). She was not to say a word for two days unless absolutely requested by the audience or her co-trainer. She had no resistance to this at all. She sat there quietly, radiating light, and was a constant source of nourishment and support to me and the group. When we finally asked her to speak, what she said was perfect. Several times I needed her to handle situations going on outside the room. She handled a very delicate problem for me in the area of religion. She told the truth to everyone at a level that was amazing.

After the training, Monday morning at sunrise, I went into Steve and Rima's room and curled up between them with the new being between and around us all. We were all in bliss, the four of us in bed.

I stayed at Rima's house
I watched her rebirth people
I watched her handle tough situations in groups
I watched her be a teacher
I let her be my teacher
I really agreed with my decision!

At the Heaven On Earth Training at the Jubilee she blew me away again when it was her hour to teach. She was very pregnant. She wore an absolutely divinely sexy outfit that totally exposed her bare belly to the group, which was around 100 people. Over the mike she guided us to lie down in groups of three. The person in the middle was to be the fetus in the womb. The two on the outside were to be the parents. We all snuggled with a lot of love. And then she put on the record "Sounds of the Womb" from Japan. For an hour she guided us through a lovely gentle warm rebirth over the mike. I cried very much. I breathed very much. I surrendered to her very much.

14

Get Clear on Money

Once I actually had a Rebirthing client who had been married to two different millionaires. They had lost all their money when they were with her. This woman was extremely intelligent and she wondered what this was about and if she had anything to do with it.

During her Rebirth I found out that her father had been very wealthy. He had made some very heavy bets at the casinos in Monte Carlo that his wife, who was expecting, was going to have a boy. When in fact, his wife delivered a baby girl, he was not only very disappointed, he lost a great deal of money. When this woman was growing up she never heard the end of this story. Her father made it very plain to her that she was the cause of him losing lots of money. He told her this so many times when she was little that she believed it and she started getting the thought in her head, "I cause men to lose lots of money." Then she, of course, attracted rich men like her father who lost money when they were with her, which proved that her father must be right and that she was in fact terrible. Of course, the men she attracted had thoughts like "Women rip me off," etc., so their patterns "dovetailed."

Money arguments are a common cause of divorce. It is all so unnecessary because it is possible to clear out the negative money karma that each person brings to a relationship.

Money is very important in a relationship. More upsets, arguments, and even divorce center around money than you can imagine, though the real cause of the conflict may often be something else.

Money is like love, in that the amount of it you have all depends on how much you are willing to receive. You will have only as much as you feel comfortable having. Therefore, don't blame others for what you don't have.

Money is also like food, because it obeys your instructions just like food does. Money is energy and you control its flow. The same is true of food. In fact, if you were not breast-fed adequately when you were an infant, you may be run by the idea that "I can't get enough" or even "I can't get any." As an adult your subconscious interprets this as "I can't get enough love" or "I can't get enough money."

It is not necessary to fight over money in your relationship. You can use a simple writing process to get clear on the negative thoughts you may have about money. Write at the top of a clean sheet of paper: "My ten most negative thoughts about money are. . ." After listing your negative thoughts, take each one and convert it into a positive affirmation. You will immediately change your results with money.

You do have a relationship with money, you know. Its presence or absence strictly follows your thoughts. You can use it to beat yourself up (just as you can use a person to beat yourself up) if you want a little disapproval.

There is really no excuse to hang around in poverty. Give yourself approval and allow the money to flow your way. Remind yourself of what Rev. Ike once told me:

GOD IS OPULENT

I once mentioned to Phil Laut* that when we conduct the Training we never mention the word *money* much, yet graduates frequently report that their incomes double after they

---

*Phil Laut, *Money Is My Friend.*

take the Training. When asked what he thought was the reason, he told them:

All the money that anyone ever received came from other people. All the money that everyone ever spent went to other people. Money is a very pervasive substance and it pervades almost every relationship that you have. This is easy to see in the relationships you have with people you live with and share expenses with, and it is easy to see in the relationships with people you work with. However, even if your relationship is limited to meeting for dinner once a month to discuss Egyptian art, your question of who will pay for the dinner probably crosses your minds. Therefore, people tend to experience greater ease and abundance in their cash flow as they experience more ease and trust in their relationships.

The LRT is based upon spiritual truth, the essence of which is the individual divinity of every person. The knowledge that you create your own reality by virtue of your personal divinity (as manifested by your ability to choose your thoughts and, in fact, change them at any time) brings the process of giving and receiving into present time. This means that patterns of obligations, guilt, and manipulation surrounding the giving and receiving of everything, including love and money, tend to drop away. For example, since I am a divine being, I have the thought of giving you something before I give it to you in every case. It follows that you must have the thought of receiving it before you do so. This makes receiving a causative act instead of a random accident over which you have no control. As long as you think that receiving obligates you or provides the giver the right to manipulate you, then it is safer to protect yourself from these unpleasant feelings by only giving, which seems to put you in control. Your willingness to receive is a service in itself; it allows the other person to give freely.

For me, the LRT was a big step in learning to trust myself. The essence of prosperity consciousness is the unconditional willingness to trust the love and generosity of other people. For almost everyone, birth was our first experience of relationships with people whom we could see, and it probably taught us that it is painful to trust other people. A key element of parental conditioning subsequent to birth is that your parents' ideas are more trustworthy than your own. This is an idea that is enforced by most parents through the practices of reward and punishment that pervade any emotional system of logic that is based upon conditional love. Loving yourself is closely akin to trusting yourself, so that the increased self-esteem that graduates experience results in increased self-trust, which then results in an increased sense of financial abundance.

We are *at ease* of receiving.

Graduates learn the art of receiving.

They remove the blocks to receiving love and therefore money also.

15

Get Clear on Sex

I once worked with a couple who had been to many prominent sex clinics. While they were there, his sex "problem" (premature ejaculation) temporarily cleared up. But when they got home, it came back and they were on the verge of divorce again. I was leaving Los Angeles in 30 minutes but when I got this call, I agreed to see him on my way to the airport. It was a shot in the dark. I made it very plain that I had very little time so he was going to have to answer my questions quickly and truthfully and he was going to have to trust me immediately. He agreed.

I went back to his first sexual experience. I found that his mother, who "knew" intuitively that *that* was going to be the night, yelled at him as he went out the door, "If you get a girl pregnant, I'll kill you!" For some reason he took it quite literally and he got the whole thing over quickly, so quickly that he did not get a chance to come inside the girl, or any other. He had never, however, made the connection between what his mother had said and what had happened. He, being very embarrassed by his first sexual disaster, decided there was something physically wrong with him, or even worse, mentally, perhaps. And then he could not perform again. I gave him a simple affirmation and asked him to promise to do it. He agreed. I asked him to write, "It is now safe for me to be inside of a woman," "I am safe when I come inside a woman," etc. At the last minute I looked at his wife and said, "For some reason, I think you should also do an affirmation and the one I think you should do is this, "I am now willing for my husband to clear up his sex problem." She amazed me by saying, "How do you know me so well?" She confessed that she was afraid that if he cleared up his premature ejaculation he would start going out with other women.

They wrote to me later saying that it worked.

Sexual problems are more complex than they may appear. Both parties are involved and it is important to find out how the patterns are intertwined. Sex "techniques" will never work permanently unless the necessary thoughts are changed.

Most of us could learn to receive a lot more pleasure than we are now experiencing. The key to this is your willingness to have it. To have a good sex life you must have a high self-esteem. If you have a low opinion of yourself you won't think you deserve sexual pleasure. Another way of looking at this is to say that you will have only as much pleasure in sex as you are willing to give yourself.

These days people have read so much about sexual technique that both men and women are self-conscious and worried about gratifying their partners. What actually works best in bed is pleasing yourself. By this I mean that the partners can make an agreement to be responsible for their own orgasms by telling each other what is most pleasurable and taking turns in giving and receiving. If you agree to be completely honest about your desires and your responses, then there is never any need to wonder about whether your partner is happy or bored, satisfied or frustrated, tired or turned on.

Of course, sexual fulfillment requires you to get rid of all your old negative thoughts about sex being dirty, dangerous, forbidden, scary, or whatever. *Sex is innocent!* It is all those old negatives we attach to it that mess us up. You can start clearing them now by writing down all your negative thoughts about sex and turning them into affirmations.

This may seem obvious, but it is very important: When you are having sex it helps to think about sex (many people actually think about the dry cleaning, the garbage, the kids, and the shopping instead). Focus your whole attention on the area of your body that is being touched. During foreplay when you are taking turns pleasuring each other, both people should be concentrating their attention on the person receiving. I focus my attention on the area of my body being touched and my partner focuses his attention on the area of my body being touched; then we switch. Two minds focused on one body make very powerful sexual energy, and sex *is* energy. The purer your energy, the purer and greater the sexual experience.

It helps to remind yourself that you can stop and talk during a sexual experience—especially if it is not going the way you want. For some reason people behave as if, once they start, they can't change it or talk about it until it is over. Communication is important. You have to learn to ask for what you like.

Some people tend to hold their breath during lovemaking. Believe me, you can take in a lot more love if you are breathing!

And it is a wonderful time to Rebirth yourself together if you have learned how to do that. Sex is totally different once you have resolved your birth trauma. For one thing, it suddenly becomes safe to let go totally; you can surrender because you know there is nothing lurking down there that is scary or sad. For another, your breathing is adjusted and you can handle a lot more energy and pleasure as a result. You can even learn to control your orgasms and make them longer by holding your breath at certain times.

16

Learn to
Handle Jealousy

Fred and Barbara were always fighting about jealousy. She claimed Fred was always interested in other women and paying more attention to them than he was to her. She said Fred was now interested in her best friend and she wanted a divorce. Fred had had one affair but stopped it when she had threatened divorce.

At first it looked as though Fred was the culprit all around. She was sure of it, of course. But when I explored their cases with more depth I found out that Barbara had a sister of whom she was insanely jealous. This sister seemed to win all the attention from their father and Barbara claimed that her father not only paid more attention to her sister than he did to her, he also gave this sister more gifts and money. Furthermore, this sister seemed to have a way with men; and men who came to visit the family always flirted with her sister instead of her.

So what Barbara had done was set up a situation where Fred became her father and all these "other women" became her sister. Then she would go into a rage, and who she was *really* angry with was her father. And when she felt like "killing" the other woman, who she really felt like killing was her own sister.

Fred had a thought that women were out to trap him. Because of Barbara's insane jealousy and possessiveness, he was sure of it. She fit his pattern. She was like his mother who was always possessive of him.

Once they saw they were trapped in patterns and that they were unconsciously trying to heal each other of old family conditions, things lightened up. Barbara finally forgave her sister and got off her resentment by discovering her own beauty and talents. Fred stopped acting out her pattern and belief systems. He confessed he really didn't want any other woman anyway. When he forgave his mother for being so possessive, Barbara also stopped acting out his belief systems and she stopped being overly possessive.

It is a rare person who has not experienced jealousy, but I have observed that the more you raise your self-esteem, the less jealousy you will have. People with high self-esteem feel centered and confident most of the time, and they know that they can be happy even when they are alone. They are aware that they can be happy without their current partner and that they can create for themselves a new and better partner if the current one goes away. People with high self-esteem know that they can get what they want, and they usually set up their lives so that there is little room for jealousy.

It constantly amazes me that people go into relationships without ever talking about their expectations regarding fidelity. At one of the first Loving Relationships Trainings, I asked the people in the room to raise their hands to indicate whether they were in strictly monogamous or open relationships. The session came unglued when several couples discovered that one partner thought their relationship was monogamous while the other thought it was open. It is pretty silly to go into a marriage without having an agreement on such a basic issue, but apparently this is exactly what happens in many cases.

There is no "right" answer to whether it is better to have a monogamous or an open relationship. The secret is to know yourself very well and find out what you can tolerate and what you can enjoy. Here are some common opinions:

1. Primary relationship, closed sexually (monogamous)

2. Primary relationship, open sexually
3. Multiple partners
4. Group marriage
5. Celibacy

It is crucial that you consider your own standards of behavior when deciding what kind of relationship is right for you. If "promiscuous" is a dirty word to you, it is not likely that having multiple partners will make you happy. If you choose a form that is not compatible with your principles you may punish yourself later. Ask yourself, "What form best suits my purposes in life?" Remember: You can be the source of your own code of ethics, "What is safe and appropriate for me, but doesn't hurt others?"

When somebody asked me how to handle jealousy, I suggested that they start by looking at why they set up a jealousy situation in the first place. In other words, what is the payoff? Are they using jealousy scenes to beat themselves up? Why do they want misery in their lives? If you find that another person is involved with the one you love, ask yourself these questions:

1. Did I attract this situation to prove I wasn't good enough?

2. Does the other woman represent my sister who got more of my father's love?

3. Does the other man represent my brother who got more of my mother's love?

4. Was my relationship getting too good and too close, so that I had to destroy it?

5. Was I getting more love than I thought I deserved, so that I had to get rid of it?

6. Am I addicted to pain, and do I secretly love it?

7. Do I think misery is the natural state?

8. Am I hooked on drama instead of peace?

9. Am I trying to prove that others are out to get me?

10. Do I think that I can never trust a man (or woman), and this proves it?

11. Do I think I can't get what I want?

12. Do I think life is a ripoff, and this proves it?

13. Do I think I can't keep what I want?

14. Am I using this mess so that I have an excuse to get rid of my partner?

15. Do I love to punish myself with this because I have guilt about something?

16. Do I secretly want to have other partners myself, and am I lying to myself?

17. Am I trying to get rid of my partner?

Do you begin to see why you can't blame others for your jealousy? You created this mess! You wanted it to prove something; you wanted to prove that your negative beliefs were right. Remember: *What you believe to be true, you create.*

When you find a person you like, explore all the feelings and beliefs you both have about relationships and then agree on the form that best suits you both. If you continue to work at mastering the suggestions in this chapter, one day you will have either:

1. A monogamous relationship in which neither of you sets up jealousy situations, or

2. An open relationship that you can handle easily without any jealousy, or

3. Some other arrangement that is a total WIN for you.

If there is one thing I have learned well from Bobby and my work it is this: There are *no shoulds;* there are *no supposed tos.* You don't have to have relationships one way or another. You don't have to be married to be OK. Just because someone else is married or in a big relationship does not make them any better than you or any worse. Just because your relationship changes does not mean life does not work for you. *You always get what you need.*

Some periods in your life you might need to be alone and that is the healthiest thing. Some periods in your life you may need to have many relationships in order to get many lessons. In some period of your life, marriage might teach you the most. You will always set it up so that you get the lessons that are important for you. You will naturally create situations that will heal you the fastest and help you to give up the ego. We have all kinds of relationships going on in the universe; they are all healing and one form is no better than another.

17

Understand Suppressed Incest

Jill told me that she and George had started out with a fabulous sex life, but as soon as they had gotten married, she suddenly got "turned off." She blamed George, but none of her reasons really seemed to make any sense. She finally admitted that herself. I asked her if this had ever happened to her before and she confessed that there was another man it happened with, and she noticed that the situation did not arise until they had moved in together. "And what was common about both of these men?" I asked her. "They each look a lot like my father," she replied. I pointed out that since these men were so much like her father, it was hard for her to let herself stay turned on to them because it would be like having incest. Why, she wanted to know, was she able to make love to them in the beginning then? Most of the incestuous feelings and connections are very suppressed at the beginning of a relationship. When she set up housekeeping, however, and moved in with someone like the parent, she was flooded with childhood memories. The constant energy exchange of living together makes childhood memories surface.

She had a hard time accepting this explanation at first because she did not want to believe that she could have been sexually attracted to her father. She did agree to take the Training and she repeated it several times. After she did the processes concerning incest and heard others talk about their feelings, she felt safe enough to let some of those memories come up. Even so, she did not believe it until her fourth Training, when she suddenly let out a loud outburst of rage and started shaking and seemed about to faint. At that moment she got in touch with the anger she felt at not being able to make love to her father. This emotional release healed her and the problem cleared up.

I have always thought it would be unethical to avoid the subject of incest in a relationship course. My research in this area has taught me that suppressed incestuous feelings affect most people's sex lives to such a degree that incest underlies many of the problems that arise.

I used to wonder why couples so often start out with a great sex life, only to find it less and less pleasurable after living together or getting married. You would think that as couples got closer and closer their sex life would improve.

In the beginning of a relationship any incestuous feelings are very deeply suppressed. However, after a couple sets up housekeeping, childhood experiences are unconsciously recreated and the mate becomes more and more like the parent we once lived with. The more the mate becomes like the parent, the less one is able to make love to him. As this unconscious connection gets stronger we are less able to make love to them because of the taboo against making love to one of your parents. Often it takes a few years for this to occur because it takes a lot of energy and love and emotion to push up suppressed material from the unconscious.

Many people "go unconscious" during the incest processes of their first LRT. They have such a charge on this area that they are afraid to look at it. Slowly they realize that the things they can't talk about are the things that run them, but sometimes people are in their third Training before they allow themselves to recall incestuous feelings.

There is a lot of unnecessary guilt about incestuous feelings. You must remember that as a baby you were a very tactile, sensual being who got touched all the time. Bathing time was a time of particular pleasure where you got touched all over your body, including your genitals. Also remember that your parents were then in their sexual prime. As an infant you found this touching wonderful, but one day it stopped suddenly without explanation. Your mind told you that you had done something wrong that made it stop, and you began to feel guilty. Early sex play with siblings may have increased the guilt, though we can see that it is only natural to want to satisfy curiosity and have pleasure at the same time.

What can you do about incest now? Examine your feelings about your parents and your brothers and sisters and acknowledge whatever you find. Recognize that you don't have to act out your feelings. We all have many feelings that we choose to do nothing about. Forgive yourself for letting incest run your life. People who have told the truth about incest in our group sessions have felt totally liberated and often later report wonderful changes in their lovemaking.

In the LRT we have special processes to release suppressed incestuous feelings. In the meantime it will be very helpful to you just to "see" that you may have your partner set up to be a substitute parent and therefore your sex life with him or her may be blocked.

18

Know the Purpose
of Your Relationship

I never started thinking much about having a purpose to anything until I went to an enlightened business school for entre-
preneurs run by my friend Marshall Thurber. The first thing
he did was to establish the purpose of the school itself. Since
we were the first graduating class, that seemed appropriate. It
was also a practice session because, we agreed, the most important thing in creating a new business is for the people involved to know the purpose for the business. And they all
should agree. And everyone should know what each word
means when the purpose is written down. We thought it was
going to be easy. It took us days and days.

After this lengthy experience, I began to understand that
everyone in a business working toward a common clear purpose they all agreed upon was the first step in teamwork and a
successful business. If my purpose in a company is totally different from another person's purpose in the company, we are
working against each other.

The first thing I did after the business school was to put the
LRT staff in a room and get clear on our purpose. It took
hours. But it was worth it. It is always worth it.

I never used to think about what I was doing in a relationship
or why I was in one and not another. I never bothered to

create a purpose for my relationship. I wandered around aimlessly with a mate I just happened to meet. I did not consciously create either the right mate or the right relationship for me.

Now that I am enlightened, I have taken great care in thinking about purpose and talking it over with my partners. I always talk about God first; before, I was terrified even to bring up that word. My purpose is to create a holy relationship to serve God together, to create the Kingdom of Heaven on earth together, and to share the light. Every man I have been with since I became enlightened has agreed to this immediately. If he didn't, I would not want him to be with me for long; anyway, I would never attract a man who did not have this same purpose, and that makes my life easy.

You can word your purpose any way that suits you. The important thing is to know what it is. This also applies to relationships other than personal ones. For instance, you may enter a business relationship strictly to earn money. But it is always good to remember to "Seek ye first the Kingdom of God and all these things shall be added unto you." If you have this purpose and, in addition, learn the game of going for the highest spiritual thought, I can assure you that things will improve rapidly in all your relationships.

The *Course in Miracles* talks about the difference between a holy relationship and an unholy one:

> . . . an unholy relationship is based on differences, where each one thinks the other has what he has not. They come together, each to complete himself and rob the other. They stay until they think there is nothing left to steal, and then they move on. And so they wander through the world strangers . . .
>
> A holy relationship starts from a different premise. Each one has looked within and seen no lack. Accepting his completion, he would extend it by joining with another, whole as himself . . . this relationship has heaven's holiness. How far from home can a relationship so like to heaven be?
>
> Think of what a holy relationship can teach!

In other words, if both of you agree to commit your friendship to "something greater" than each of you, you will have tremendous spiritual force backing you up.

19

Treat Each Other with Utmost Kindness

My mother once looked me in the eyes as she asked, "Why is it that families, where people should treat each other the best, sometimes treat each other the worst?" I was unable to answer her question, but I always remembered it. We had been somewhat irritable with one another, which happened rarely. Why didn't we *always* handle our problems gently and with utmost kindness, she was more or less asking me. I was young and I wondered why she was asking *me*.

But as I grew up and traveled around the world, I was in many homes where it appeared the family members hated each other. They seemed out to get each other. They seemed like they couldn't wait to put each other down. They seemed like they would just as soon beat each other up. They seemed like their favorite way to communicate was to be sarcastic or to yell. I could never understand this. And then one day I read that most murders are committed right in the home! I was appalled.

I went to a home one day where the only one that got treated decently was the dog. I always wondered why this was, just like my mother wondered.

The research we have done for the LRT has shed some light. Most people are angry at their parents and they are taking it out on their mates. They aren't even relating to the person they are living with. They are relating to someone the person is set up to be. When you clean up this anger with your parents (and you need to do this whether they are dead or alive), then you can start relating to your mate as a friend that you will treat like an angel.

It may seem silly to have to be told this if you are an adult. But really, how often have you forgotten to do this? Perhaps we do have to be reminded of the Golden Rule.

It is possible to live by the Golden Rule even when the other person is totally upset and angry. The first thing to remember is to just let them express their anger without getting yourself into it. Inside every scream there is a message. They are asking you for help and they don't know how to put it.

Here are some simple recommendations:

1. Remember not to "match energies."

2. Remember to breathe; help them to breathe deeply also.

3. Offer your love by asking, "How can I support you?"

4. Suggest ways to work out anger elsewhere if appropriate.

5. Be willing to *listen* right now.

As the *Course In Miracles* states: Every loving thought is true. Everything else is an appeal for help or healing.

Meditate on the idea of treating your mate and family members as if they were kings and queens. Isn't that how you would like to be treated? Meditate on the idea of treating them like a saint. See the divinity in everyone and then they will start acting divine around you.

20

Learn to Use "Imaging"

One day one of my friends showed up with a beautiful blonde he was madly in love with. "How did you find her?" I asked him. He told me it was quite simple. He merely wrote down exactly all the qualities he wanted in a woman, got a picture of her in his mind, and imagined it daily until one day she "showed up."

One day I met a fabulous man in New York City with whom I still have a great relationship. I came out of the shower and I had towels wrapped around me. I was visiting friends who had some of my books for sale. This man had come over to buy one. I looked at him and he looked at me and the connection was instant. Later when we went out together he told me that he had spent quite a bit of time "imaging me" and meeting me. He had spent quite a while focusing on my picture on the back of my first book. He did not know where he would meet me or when, but he was certain he could and would meet me. He had not known I was in town that day. But there we were suddenly in a little hallway together.

So you see, imaging *works*.

What you think of yourself, what you say about yourself, what you believe to be true about yourself—will manifest.

As a man thinketh in his heart, so is he. —*Proverbs*

It is a universal law that you will create what you believe to be true: The thinker is creative. So if you continually think of yourself as all messed up, that is the way you will stay. "But I *am* messed up," you might protest. The answer to that is the resolve to change your picture of yourself through affirmations and imaging.

Imaging is the process of seeing something just the way you want it to be. If you take time each day to create images in your mind of the ideal you, your mind will begin to create that ideal in reality. Start seeing yourself anew. See yourself healed and imagine what that would be like. See your relationships just the way you want them, all healed and working perfectly. See yourself as young, beautiful, successful, and emotionally and physically healthy.

If you have difficulty with imaging, it may be because you were told as a child that daydreaming is bad. Well, daydreaming about success and happiness is not only OK, it is downright good for you!

The sports world has adopted imaging quite successfully. Golfers spend hours imaging perfect shots and when they get on the course success seems only natural. Skiers have done the same thing.

Imaging is a very pleasant way to spend time, and it is positively creative in its results.

Another way to image what you want is to make a treasure map, a visual tool to facilitate what you want in manifested form. Cut out pictures that represent your desired result and paste them on colored poster board. On the board, include the Cosmic Clause:

THIS OR SOMETHING BETTER
NOW MANIFESTS FOR ME
IN TOTALLY HARMONIOUS WAYS WITH
GOOD FOR ALL CONCERNED.

21

Learn to Use a Mantra

Once, after splitting up with a man I loved, I drove myself nuts thinking about him. It seemed like all I could think about was him; and everytime I thought about it, I felt pain. The more I tried *not* to think about him, the more I thought about him. Nothing seemed to work. It seemed like I could not get him out of my mind. The problem got worse and worse. It seemed like I could not think of *anything* else!

Fortunately, I was heading for Campbell Hot Springs and Diane Hinterman was there. We crawled in bed together and stayed up all night talking. She told me tales of India and Babaji and I was thrilled. I, somewhat embarrassed to put it mildly, finally got around to telling her about my "preoccupation." She gave me a simple answer. She told me to say a mantra every time the thought of that man and our relationship came up. I tried it and it worked. (By the way, now I am very glad it turned out the way it did.)

Think about God as often as you can, especially when things get rough in your relationship. The Science of Mind Church has a technique called the "Golden Key" that is wonderful and simple. Everytime you catch yourself indulging in worry about a problem in your life, *stop,* and think about God instead. Remember that one of the important universal laws is "What you think about expands." If you dwell on a problem, you will get more of it and it will get worse. If you dwell on your idea of God, you will be filled with that.

If there is no concept of God that works for you, try saying a *mantra*—words or syllables that you chant so that the sound will still your mind. The one that Babaji taught was "Om Namaha Shivai," which has many meanings. The translation I like best is "Infinite Being, Infinite Intelligence, and Infinite Manifestation." Saying a mantra will get you clear of habitual negative thought patterns and will also bring you peace and joy.

An affirmation is a kind of mantra. Chanting to yourself an affirmation, like "I am increasing my willingness to be loved," is effective and gets you very high.

22

Have the
Right Attitude

One night Bill Chappelle and I were doing a Training at a hotel in San Francisco. We were both complaining about one thing or another. I don't even remember what the situation was, but we were into an attitude of gloom for some reason. I said, "Look, Bill, Kyle said I should definitely read this book, so why don't we do it right now? I'll read it to you aloud." He said, "Great." At that point *anything* would have felt better than what we were feeling. As it turned out, we stayed up all night and took turns reading the book to each other. Our attitude about everything totally changed. We got so high that we could not sleep. We were soaring!

Watch your attitude.

A wonderful little book, *The Door of Everything*, channeled by Ruby Nelson, talks about the "Ascension" attitudes. These attitudes will bring you good relationships, and they will also thrust you into an altogether fabulous life. The Ascension attitudes are *Love, Praise* and *Gratitude*. If your being radiates these attitudes, you will easily attract all the wonderful friends and mates you could ever want.

Giving thanks for the good things you have always brings you more good things. Many people spend time focusing on what they don't have. Every time I have focused on a lack for any length of time it has led me into misery. Catherine Ponder, in discussing the principle of giving thanks, says that your highest good is there for you, even if you are not experiencing it yet. Give thanks that your perfect mate is there for you in the universe, and admit that you have not been ready to receive. God is ready when you are.

The Source thrives on having you receive from it, because the giver always expands by the giving. So don't block the things you deserve to receive and don't block the love that is there for you. In the same way, if you lose something, know that it was no longer best for you, and that the Source is clearing the way to give you something even greater.

If you focus on loss you'll get more loss. If you give thanks for what you have, you'll get more.

I always try to have the attitude that whatever happens is the perfect thing to happen. Even if it seems "bad" at first, I always know there is a lesson there and it probably happened so I could get the lesson. I always manage to turn everything into a "win." This attitude I never lose and I stay happy.

23

Master the
Five Biggies

This is probably one of the most important chapters in the book. Read it very carefully and think about the ideas a long time.

Before I became aware of this information, my life did not work very well. After I became aware of this information and started handling it, my life started working really well. Need I say more? I am sure every Rebirther would agree and I am sure everyone else who has cleared these points would agree. So please, for your own sake, do not take this chapter lightly. Think about it. Take action on it. You will be *so* relieved if you do.

The "Five Biggies" are negative consciousness factors that affect most people and keep them from experiencing bliss. They were brilliantly conceived by Leonard Orr; I have adapted them specifically to relationships for the Training. The five biggies are:
  1. The birth trauma
  2. The parental disapproval syndrome
  3. Specific negatives
  4. The unconscious death urge
  5. Other lifetimes

We have talked about the way your birth affects your relationships extensively in other parts of this book.

The *parental disapproval syndrome* is about how parents invalidate their children the way they themselves were invalidated. These invalidations break the spirit of the child and the child loses self-esteem and sells out its power. We grow up so used to disapproval that we unconsciously set up our partners to give us more of the same. This syndrome alone wipes us out, and we are always feeling hurt by the disapproval we create. Our mates become our disapproving parents, and we end up eventually having to divorce our "parents."

In the Training we take a great deal of time to clear out the parental disapproval syndrome from people's consciousness. On the first day we dissolve it as much as possible so that the next day there is space in which to create a new kind of relationship, a new kind of love. First we clean house and then we decorate, and both turn out to be fun.

Specific negatives are negative thought structures that you carry around about yourself and about life. These are affecting your relationships constantly. If you have a negative thought from birth, for example, it is easy to see how that has affected results all your life. We have already seen how affirmations clear up negatives.

A *personal law* is your most negative thought about yourself. Let's imagine that yours is "I never get what I really want." Upon this you would therefore have built many negative beliefs.

The worst part about your personal law is that you are unconsciously putting out a command to the universe telepathically whether you speak or not. In the case above, you would be putting out: "People! Don't give me what I want!" Others would have to respond to you appropriately. If you didn't know you had this personal law (most people don't), then you might wonder why others get what they want and you don't.

It is very important to understand how the *unconscious death urge* affects your relationships. Most people have the thought that there is a source outside themselves that is going to kill them. We are finally enlightened enough to take responsibility for facing the truth that *all death is suicide*. If you completely accept the law that the thinker creates with his thoughts, then you know you can change the thought that death is inevitable: "I can keep my body as long as I want and I can also tell my cells to *youth* instead of age."

Becoming enlightened increases your energy tremendously, and all that energy provides more power to all your thoughts. You must give up the thought that death is inevitable or all your new energy will lead you to kill yourself faster. Many great people died young because they were unable to comprehend this.

In a mortal relationship you are always attached to the umbilical cord of death. You constantly worry that your mate may die and leave you all alone, maybe even to die alone. Pain and separation are imminent, fear or even terror of surrender is present, and death is lurking. If you decide that you can't trust a God who is out to destroy you in the end, then you will have little reason to trust ordinary people, including your own mate. There is often an underlying attitude that "If I have to die, I'll make sure he or she will die too." So your partner's death urge can suck you in, or vice versa. Two people marching to the grave together in pain, misery, and sorrow is not what I have in mind for a loving relationship.

Life in an immortal relationship is totally different. It starts with the premise that you are forever there for each other and that your relationship is eternal, though it will be continuously transforming. It might be in one form for a few years and in another form some other time; but it is always there and always healing and loving. There is no fear of surrender because of this. There is a pervasive sense of well-being. Bliss, peace, joy, happiness, and fun are abundant.

Other lifetimes sometimes exert a strongly negative influence on our present lives. You can clear this up with specialists in past-life regressions if you need extra help. We have found, however, that if you just clear up everything in this life right down to conception (it is possible to remember conception during rebirthing) it will generally free you from any karma you may have been worried about.

24

Use Your Relationships for Enlightenment

After I got divorced and was "hurt" a few more times, I decided maybe I should avoid relationships. They seemed to be destroying me. And I noticed that many of my friends had decided the same thing. You may have decided that too, after being brokenhearted, banged up, hurt, disappointed, devastated, left broke, feeling half-dead, and a nervous wreck over relationships.

My trouble was that I did not know how to use relationships for enlightenment and for healing myself. I didn't, quite frankly, know what was going on. Now I know no one can hurt me but myself. I know that if I feel hurt, there is something I have not cleared. I know that if a man leaves, someone greater is coming along. I know that there is a new way to handle relationships a way that *always* brings me peace and joy and enlightenment no matter *what* happens. You, too, can have this resolution. You and your partner can learn to get the maximum joy and value out of your relationship no matter how it turns out. You can even part and feel good about it. You can even get *exactly* what you desire in a relationship.

A partner will bring up all your patterns. Don't avoid relationships; they are the best seminar in town. The truth is that *your partner is your guru.* Because they help you to get healed, you should always be thankful to your mates for serving you. Remember, you created them in your life, so don't resent them when you get into upsets.

You could have the greatest mate ever and still set it up so that you don't win. It is so important to set up your relationship on a win basis. You have to like yourself a lot to let yourself win all the time. Most people like to beat themselves up, and it is easy to use a relationship to prove that you are no good. But that same relationship can offer the perfect opportunity for you to say yes to life and health. The opportunity is always there; it's up to you to do something with it.

Your results are also your guru. You can look out there every second and see from your results how your mind is operating on every level. Children also clearly reflect the state of your own consciousness. They continually act out the subconscious minds of their parents. When the kids are screaming around you, don't yell at them, but go off into another room and see what part of your suppressed negative mass they want to help you release. *Children are your guru,* and parents who know that are wonderful with their kids. Children will always act out your negatives so you can see them more clearly.

Remember, you are always in a relationship with yourself in the presence of another. Acknowledge and thank the other person for serving as a mirror. One definition of a loving relationship I like is "When one partner does not interfere with the other's love for himself" (Kyle Os).

25

Give Each Other Space

Once I was "playing around," designing a house that would most enhance a healthy relationship. What I came up with, to my surprise, was a house that had a master bedroom where the couple slept together, and adjoining on each side, his and her private sanctuaries, also with beds where each could retreat to. No one else was allowed to enter. This was a total, I mean *total*, private space. For me, of course, it would be ideal. I could go into that room and write books and never be bothered. I would think that everyone should have somewhere to go where they could be *totally* alone. Think about it.

It is important to set up your relationship so that each of you has time alone without the other feeling rejected and hurt. In this way you can maintain your independence and creativity without developing secret resentment. Allowing yourself time alone each day with the Source is one of the most important things you can do; people unfortunately tend to put that time last or to skip it completely. Since you are basically an ethical person, sooner or later your thirst for God and hunger for spiritual food will be great enough that you might want to get rid of a mate who seems to take you away from your most creative divine states.

You don't have to get rid of someone in order to have space; you merely have to make the space for yourself. Set up your relationship in the beginning so that it is natural to be alone certain hours of the day or week. When you can live with yourself, you can live with others.

Each of us has talents that we long to express. Talents are of no value to anyone, certainly not to you, if you don't use them. You will also start hating yourself, feeling guilty, and maybe take this out on your mate.

You don't have to go to a different state or country in order to be alone; distance doesn't matter. It is good to have a room all to yourself, but if that is not possible you can always take an early morning walk or sit in a park or a church. Often when I am on the road I do not have any place to be alone. I have re-solved this in various ways, sometimes getting up at 4 A.M. to get out and enjoy the sunrise on my own. The bathroom is a very good place to be alone because people generally respect your privacy there. Taking a long bath is a wonderful oppor-tunity to be alone and meditate. My favorite way to be alone is to go under water and breathe through a snorkel in a bath or hot tub. I always travel with a snorkel in my briefcase. (This form of wet Rebirthing should not be attempted alone, how-ever, until you've mastered dry Rebirthing with a Rebirther.)

Being alone is frightening to some people because they are afraid of their own thoughts and of God and death. Once you are clear that you can change your thoughts with affirmations and that there is no Source outside yourself that can kill you, it is wonderful to be alone.

I got clear on this by locking myself in a room for four days and four nights. (You don't have to go to India to find your-self.) I deliberately chose a remote place on an island with no room service and no phone. I took no food, only a little juice. I had no TV, no magazines, no radio, not even any writing materials.

The first day I just sat on the bed and watched all my gar-bage thoughts run amok. I felt like I was sitting in a pool of garbage. The second day I received a mantra that I recited. It

brought up a lot of hate that I had stored since I was a child—
hatred for God for killing people (or so it seemed to me) and
especially for killing my father.

I finally came up with an affirmation: "I forgive myself for
hating God for what I did or for what others did to themselves." I cleaned up my relationship with God. The next day I
went into a meditative state. It was so pleasurable that at the
time I could only handle that much pleasure for a short time.

Since that four-day experience I often pray and talk out
loud to God when I am alone. This is very effective, and very
emotional, I might add. Prayer, by the way, is when you talk
to God, and meditation is when God talks to you. It feels good
to be in a constant state of prayer and meditation.

26

Surrender Yourself

When I started getting Rebirthed, I soon learned that the answer to it all was to totally surrender. I could easily see that the people who surrendered went into bliss and the people who resisted went into pain. Life is like that. Relationships are like that. I remember Leonard once saying to me that people who had the ability to totally surrender did not go into paralysis in Rebirthing. I never went into paralysis in Rebirthing, although sometimes it was very close. During those times I just kept saying to myself, "I surrender. I will not resist God." I have found that in relationships it is hard to surrender totally unless you have unconditional love and trust going. I have noticed that it is easier to surrender to someone who has worked out the "five biggies" and is into positive thinking. When you feel really safe, it is easier to surrender. Of course, you must create safety in your own mind. This is easier to do around a safe and loving person.

Meditate on the word *surrender*.

Surrender.
Surrender to God.
Surrender to your mate.
Surrender to the highest spiritual thought.

Surrender is not a form of behavior. It is an openness and a willingness to receive.

Surrender is giving up control but not losing power. It does not mean giving up your power to another person; on the contrary, it is an act made to increase your own power. This is because when you are willing to receive, you are taking in more love, and when you are taking in more love, you are taking in more independence, more freedom, and more God. Power comes from love, safety, certainty, and surrender to God.

People sometimes have trouble understanding the concept that a relationship can bring you freedom. The fear of being trapped and smothered comes mostly from the birth trauma. A loving relationship can help to heal the birth trauma because the love pushes out the trauma. You can also feel trapped or smothered because of your thoughts. A relationship will heal those thoughts by bringing them to the surface and exposing them to love. Any time you are giving up thoughts to death and negativity you will feel freer and freer. They may never have come out of you if you did not let someone love you deeply.

In other words, only true freedom is freedom from death and negativity. Since the love in a relationship will heal you of these things if you let it and play the game right, it follows that a relationship can be freeing rather than constricting.

The more negativity I give up the freer I am.

The love in a relationship always helps me to release negativity and therefore I am more free.

27

"First-Aid"
for Your Relationship

Sometimes I have thought that I learned all the wrong things in school. Nobody ever taught me much about relationships: How to choose a mate, how to handle upsets, what to expect in marriage, what to do when things go nuts, how to prevent divorce, how to handle sex and/or sex problems, how to raise children wisely and all that kind of stuff I really needed to know. Later, when I went for help on these matters as an adult, it was like the blind leading the blind. Oh, how I wished I had had a few classes on these subjects rather than all that chemistry, which was helping me not at all! It seemed crazy to me that people needed licenses to drive a car, when they needed no license to be a parent, even if they were unfit to raise a child. I wondered what the world would be like if everyone had to wait until they were at least 25 to get married and everyone had to take courses in enlightened child-raising and pass a few tests on that subject before they were allowed to have a child.

   Well, the best I could hope for was a few pointers of "first-aid" techniques, for patching up relationships. I couldn't find them anywhere either. And after my marriage fell apart and I was getting a divorce and my hair was falling out and I felt like killing myself and I found nobody to help me that made any

sense, I decided I was going to have to figure it out on my own.
I feel I have done that in my own way. It was a struggle, however, and if I can save you any time, I would like to do that. I
may have to go through a great deal more before I figure out
the easiest way.

*What to do when it looks like your relationship is falling apart
and you both want to stay together and get it to work.*

First, remember that the relationship *is* working if you
both want to stay together; you are just temporarily locked
into a heavy pattern. By now you know that what is happening
between the two of you is happening to heal you of something.
The love between the two of you is pushing out some negative
mental mass. Another way of putting this is that your patterns
are "dovetailing." Instead of yelling and screaming at one
another, take one of these alternatives:

1. Consult with someone you trust.

2. Call your local Rebirther and make an appointment.

3. Write down all your negative thoughts and turn them
into affirmations.

4. Become aware of all the blame thoughts you have about
the other. Remember that blame is always off the track. All
disapproval comes from a corner of your own mind; your partner is your mirror. What does this say about you? How did you
create this? How did you attract this?

5. Remember that love is bringing up things unlike itself.
Don't leave until you understand the pattern at least, or you
will just recreate it with the next person.

6. Handle your anger in individually appropriate ways.

7. Remember that you are never upset for the reason that
you think. Get in touch with the earlier situation you are reliving.

8. Lie down and hold each other. When you can't communicate, *stop* and hold each other and breathe together gently.

9. When you have calmed down, share all feelings, one at
a time. One person talks, the other listens without interrupt-
ing.

10. Review the LRT or take the advanced Training.

If your mate is with another woman or another man and you are blaming them both, *stop*. Sit down alone and tell yourself the truth. Try writing the following phrases at the top of a piece of paper and see how many things you can list for each one.

    1. The reasons I attracted this situation are . . .

    2. My payoff for creating this mess is . . .

    3. What I get to prove to myself is . . .

    4. What that other person represents is . . .

    5. The reasons I secretly want my mate to do this are . . .

    6. The thoughts I have been thinking that created this are . . .

    7. The thoughts I need to think to clear up my jealousy are . . . . Since your partner is your mirror, it is possible that you, yourself, secretly want to go out with someone else. Maybe you have resented knowing that others have the pleasure you won't allow yourself to have. Or, you may be pulling in another person who represents one of your siblings who took away the attention of one of your parents (i.e. you are setting up your partner as your parent).

If the relationship falls apart despite everything you have tried to do, and your partner leaves you, remember this: You never lose anything or anyone who was with you for your highest good under any circumstances. If it seems that you have lost someone, then that person was no longer for your highest good.

The best news of all is this: Nothing is ever taken from you without its being replaced by something greater. In this situation, God is trying to give you something better, so *let go*. You must create a vacuum to receive the new.

ALL LOSSES ARE
GAINS NOT RECOGNIZED

Affirmations Worksheet

My most negative thoughts about relationships are:

_____

_____

_____

_____

_____

_____

My most negative thoughts about myself are:

_____

_____

_____

_____

_____

_____

My most negative thoughts about men are:

_____

_____

_____

_____

_____

_____

My most negative thoughts about women are:

_____

_____

_____

_____

_____

_____

My new affirmations about relationships are:

_____

_____

_____

_____

_____

_____

My new affirmations about myself are:

_____

_____

_____

_____

_____

_____

My new affirmations about men are:

_____

_____

_____

_____

_____

_____

My new affirmations about women are:

_____

_____

_____

_____

_____

_____

PART TWO

More About Relationships

28

Troubleshooters

Note this:
When you finally give up a pattern
    you might feel sad
    you might feel lonely
    you might feel confused and uncertain
    you might feel lost
    you might even "miss" that negative mental mass
    you might feel it is like a "little death."

This will pass.

Don't fill that void with another problem.
Fill it with love.

Also:
If love makes you mad or sad, then you might not let yourself
have much (or any).

Love is innocent
Accept this concept; otherwise you might have long
periods of being mad or sad.

The same thing is true for money.

Money is innocent

Clear away *things* you have attached to the words *love* and *money;* separate the chaff from the grain. Then take your pick.

Furthermore:

If you are afraid and you suppress it, you will just create more scary things and become even more afraid, because

What you fear you attract.

The way out of fear is to let yourself *feel* it and talk about it; in this way you can "experience it out."

It is safe to feel your fear

That's why, as Bobby would say:

"Fear forward." Study your fear, feel it, let go of it. Stuffing it makes you more scared. Remember the affirmation: "I'm safe and immortal right now!"

Now note this:

Chances are, you have used one of the following to beat yourself up with:

Sex
  Love
    Money
      Your body
        Your career
          Your car.

Have you, or are you, using these things in some way to hurt yourself?

Why?

Why are you thinking you are so guilty?

Forgive yourself!

Instead of destroying yourself with those things,

Destroy guilt!

And then:

When sad,
        let yourself feel it,
                cry;

When angry,
        let yourself feel it,
                shout;

When afraid
        let yourself feel it,
                tremble;

When happy
        let yourself feel it,
                laugh;

        Feel
           Feel
Express   Feel
   Express   Feel
    Express   Feel
     Express   *Feel!*
    Express
    Express!

Try this:

When you have a problem in your relationships that occupies your mind over and over and over and causes you to worry and worry and worry . . .

Stop
THINK ABOUT GOD INSTEAD

Immediately — Give thanks it is over.

And try this:

When you feel you are ready to meet a new mate:

1. Love yourself
2. Praise God
3. Relax
4. Be happy
5. Keep your heart soft and open
6. Sing affirmations to yourself
7. Be in love with life
8. Smile
9. Breathe a lot
10. Give thanks
11. Stay in certainty
12. Stay "in love" all the time.

Then someone will surely show up!

P.S. As my friend, Bill Chapelle, would say,
"Doubt is *out!*
Intuition is *in!*"

Finally, try this:

When you feel unloved, start loving yourself and
    then go out and love someone.

When you feel unappreciated start appreciating yourself and
    then go out and appreciate someone.

When you feel unacknowledged, start acknowledging yourself
and
    then go out and acknowledge someone.

When you feel untouched, start touching yourself and
    then go out and touch someone.

When you feel ignored, start noticing yourself, and
    then go out and notice someone.

When you feel rejected, start accepting yourself, and
    then go out and accept someone.

When you feel alone, find yourself and
    then go out and find someone.

When you feel poor, start giving to yourself and
    then go out and give to someone.

And *then* you will find someone who loves you, appreciates you, acknowledges you, touches you, notices you, accepts you, finds you and gives to you.

In other words, when you feel awful . . .
    Change your thoughts;
        Love yourself — love others;
            Give to yourself — give to others;
And if all else fails . . .

Talk to God, out loud!

29

My Relationship to the LRT

The Loving Relationship Training is pure pleasure to me—it has never been work. Everyone wants to know how I created the LRT, and I find it harder to talk about how I did it than it was to actually do it. I am a little embarrassed that it was so easy. In fact, I enjoyed creating the LRT so much that I do not recall a single moment's struggle or effort. I had a few fears, that's for sure, but work it was not. It took me awhile, however, to get my personal life to go "easy." I feel God gave the LRT to me when I was ready to receive it. Of course, I had learned very well from some great teachers: Werner Erhard, Leonard Orr, Bobby Birdsall, Babaji, my mother, and every one of my lovers.

I was Leonard's chauffeur at first; later I lived in his house and he taught me Rebirthing. He taught me very well and I learned very well, and it was out of my work in Rebirthing and all the research we did into the birth trauma that the LRT was created.

My Rebirthing clients taught me constantly as I saw their entire lives unfold. When I saw how their births affected their relationships I was totally blown away. There I was, walking around with all this profound information (somehow I remembered everything they said and felt) and I just put it together, along with things I had been taught and things I had learned from the school of hard knocks. Part of the form of the Training came from my first great teacher, Werner Erhard, creator of *est*, and the data came to me from meditations, Rebirthings, and from the first graduates. Books helped me very little, my Master's degree scarcely at all. Twenty-five years of traveling around the world contributed a lot; I had been in search of the truth for a long time.

My divorce may have been the catalyst. I wanted to heal myself so that I would never go through anything like that again. My husband was a genius and we had a fabulous time together. We loved each other totally and when it ended neither of us knew why. It took me years to recover and I vowed it would never take me as long to recover from anything again.

Having been a nurse for many years, I knew that I was certainly not the only one in trouble and pain over relationships. I used to ask my patients to tell me just when their symptoms began and what was going on in their lives at the time. Invariably their physical ailments developed after an upset in their relationships—a broken romance, a divorce, or some such thing. I decided to do something about this data, but getting a degree in family sociology turned out to be irrelevant. Then one day I was led to Leonard Orr, who told me about the "five biggies." I understood them very quickly and began to see ways to apply them to my research in relationships.

And so I put myself on the line. At the time I was in my first pure relationship with a man, which I attribute to having cleared myself through Rebirthing. The man was Marshall Summers and I lived with him for two years while we studied with Leonard. It was a beautiful experience, but after awhile I found myself unable to continue receiving all that love; I was still not completely cleared. Marshall and I parted peacefully and went separate ways—he to write music and I off to India. Marshall did help me create the beginnings of the LRT and it came out of the space of our personal loving relationship for which I wish to continually acknowledge him.

Marshall and I traveled to Honolulu to do some Rebirthing workshops together, and we took with us an outline for a one-day seminar called "Loving Relationships" that we presented to thirty of our friends there. They begged us to stay longer and do it again with their friends, so we did. All of them said the same thing: "This is wonderful, but it is far too much for one day." Back in San Francisco, we tried a two-day "dry run" with friends at Theta House. I couldn't believe they all loved it so much when I felt I didn't know what I was doing. Marshall, who is a musician, sang a lot and that helped. The most unnerving moments came when we reached the jealousy section and all hell broke loose. Somehow the people favoring monogamy ended up on one side of the room and those favoring open relationships on the other. They glared at each other as if ready to kill! It was awful. After that I tore up the whole jealousy section, which continues to be touchy; by now I have rewritten it thirteen times.

One day a friend, Roger Lane, came from Hawaii to take the seminar. By then we had started to do it in a hotel with the help of a wonderful man, Michael George Fatjo, who began to organize for us. Roger was so in love with the whole thing that he began to think about moving to San Francisco so he would never have to be away from the people in his first LRT. I knew he did not really want to leave Hawaii, so I said we would bring it there if he got his island friends together. That is how it began to spread.

There were some very shaky moments in the beginning. One day I was experiencing so much jealousy myself that I was shaking throughout the Training. Though I felt inadequate to teaching just then, I decided simply to tell the truth about what I was experiencing. Because people are telepathic they would have known anyway. Leonard had told me, "Sondra, what you try to hide in the closet will be shouted from the housetops," so I decided that I would be the one on the housetops shouting about myself. People loved me for telling the truth.

In the beginning, some of the roughest times for me would

be when my own relationships would go through changes in public. It was embarrassing to be in the public eye with my private life. But in my heart I knew that "We teach what we need to learn the most," and finally I didn't care what anyone said or did. I was going to learn everything I could about how to have perfect relationships if it took me forever. If I had to go through more relationship changing—which I did—that was OK. I saw eventually that each relationship was better than the last, and I got over my embarrassment because none of my friends were doing any better and they appreciated the hell out of me for putting it on the line.

Nothing prepared me, however, for the massive amounts of energy charges I had to take through my body when a large group would start releasing the negative mental mass they had been carrying around for years. Before I became clear enough to let it flow right through me, I often had to spend the breaks Rebirthing myself. I noticed that the more I Rebirthed myself and the clearer I got, the more people would let go in my presence, and soon I had a new problem.

People in the Training would sometimes go into a spontaneous Rebirth (most often during the jealousy or incest sections). The first time it happened Marshall and I had to stop everything and Rebirth them in front of the others. Then those watching got activated and the situation bordered on bedlam. After that I made sure that there were assistants present who were good Rebirthers, so if anyone went into a spontaneous Rebirth they could just be Rebirthed in the back and I could keep right on going. This never really interfered, though it probably seemed pretty strange to some first-time participants. Actually, everyone in the room can let go better if someone is breathing a lot instead of "stuffing it."

There have been many funny and embarrassing moments in my career as an LRT trainer. The most embarrassing came when a young man shared some of the most intimate details about his sex life that I had ever heard. The room got very hot. As I stood up to comment, my red silk gaucho pants literally fell down. Marshall almost fell out of his chair laughing – in fact, you might say it brought the house down.

During a Training in Boston, Bobby and I gave a pillow to someone to help him get out his anger. He slammed it against a post several times and suddenly it exploded. The room filled with goose feathers and we could barely breathe. All of us headed for the exits, but Bobby and I ran out the fire exit and it locked behind us. We were out there on a ledge for quite a while before the laughter subsided and people began to wonder where we were and found us. (Now we use professional, padded "boffing sticks.")

Bobby and I always tried to maintain the motto "More fun per hour." Finally I was able to do the whole Training without any tension in my body no matter *what* went on in the room. I thought I might get tired of it all, but a new magic always happens. Besides, I never get tired of the truth and I never get tired of spiritual healing.

The Training is about all aspects of relationships and people say it covers everything they ever wanted to know about relationships and love. Since relationships are all there is, the Training is about all of life.

Graduates of the Training kept telling me that they had a great desire to be with me after the Training. This started me thinking about an Advanced Training which would be all experiential and give me the chance to be with the people I love. This was even easier to create than the LRT itself.

The first time we tried it was on the island of Maui in Hawaii. About thirty graduates lived together for three days and nights in a luxurious inn. There was so much love and appreciation going on around me that I was overwhelmed, and Sunday morning during breakfast my whole body began to vibrate intensely and I went into a state of altered consciousness. At one point I felt the presence of beings greater than I could comprehend. I wept unashamedly for an hour. After this experience I lost the outline for the Advanced Training, and none of the other trainers could find theirs, either. The second time I did the Advanced Training something similar happened, and I stopped doing it for a long time. I was afraid of that much rapid movement. However, after being with high-energy people I learned to handle huge amounts of love and energy better than before, and because of the continued demand I started doing them again. Now I look forward to them more than ever, since we do these seminars at very luxurious resorts where graduates have the additional opportunity to increase their prosperity consciousness. We try to hold the Advanced LRT in a resort with hot springs for wet Rebirthing.

You could say I created the LRT to heal myself, which is true; however, on a spiritual level I must have known it was my life's mission from the time I was born. After thirty-four long years I "remembered" it. The LRT came to me right after I had been writing the affirmation "I am now willing for the divine plan of my life to manifest." And it was not a coincidence that after four years of Rebirthing myself I recalled the predominant thought I had had in the womb: "When I come out everyone is going to fall in love." Indeed, my birth (I was born on the kitchen table) was a great social event in the tiny village where my parents lived, and that positive expectation from my days in the womb has led me to do a work in which people fall in love with me and each other all the time.

Since my first visit to India and my meeting Babaji, I have been focused much more on matters of the spirit. I am filled with an attitude of praise and gratitude; my heart has been opened wide and is ready to be filled with light. My one goal has been to live upward so that I can express the Spirit perfectly. I have prayed to be an authentic teacher of the Truth. God's voice sometimes vibrates through me like music. I am intoxicated with God's guidance and my body has channeled incredible amounts of purifying energy and the breath of the Spirit. Sometimes this is still a little embarrassing to me.

When Bill Chappelle asked me just how I would like to start a book on relationships, I said, "I should start with God. There is no other way. I tried everything else." However, I was still a little afraid to talk about God. I knew that many people were sick of the old concept of God. Most of the people of my generation had had it. They had looked at the God of their parents and at their parents' lives, and they said, "If that's what God does for you, I want no part of it." And most left home and left God and did not go back.

Besides people often become nervous wrecks wondering when God is going to get them. They have always hated God for putting them in a universe where there is no way to get out alive. But even when I was confused about God, I kept on going. Then I went to India to find answers and got even more confused, but I remembered Werner Erhard saying, "Confusion is a high state," and Leonard Orr saying, "Confusion is just when you have two realities at once, the old and the new." Even when things were at the most confused point, I knew that I would come out OK. I knew that I had released enough negative mental mass that I was down to the last heavy pieces. Those heavy thoughts came up and out even though my business almost blew up and I made some poor financial decisions and everything got shaky. Even then the LRT roared on; it was unsinkable no matter how I tried to sabotage it. I had created an immortal product.

When Bobby appeared and became my manager, committed to me and to the LRT forever, I figured I must surely be doing something right.

The greatest reinforcement of my self-esteem came when Babaji chose a Hindu name for me that first night in the temple. "Durkuli is your name," he said. I asked the translator what it meant. She replied, "It means 'Strong One,' 'Immortal One,' 'Everlasting One.' And, he also said that your determination is so great that you will get whatever you want even unto the ends of the earth."

30

Cleaning Up My Relationships

Once you recognize all the things that can come up to block a desirable relationship, you will find it helpful to go back to those situations and acknowledge the reasons for their failure. The most effective way I have found to clear these problems from current and future relationships is to address an open letter to those whom I loved, those who loved me, but with whom I was unable to expand the relationship.

To all the men I have loved greatly and those who have loved me:

> I am sorry for all the time I kept you out of my life or got rid of you for a long period just because of some crummy suppressed thought I had buried since birth. I know that these thoughts were so deep and strong and negative that eventually you could not endure my seemingly fruitless struggles with them. I am sorry that I wasn't aware of these thoughts sooner; I now know it was a source of hurt in my life and yours.
>
> I also know that at times you acted out those thoughts for me so I could see them more clearly. Often I did not recognize them until long after you had left. Because love takes the negative upon itself so you can see it more clearly, I can see now how you were trying to heal me by giving me the behavior I most expected. Since I did not under-

stand then, I could not acknowledge you; all I could see was my own hurt and I was stuck in blame. As long as I blamed you I did not have to take responsibility for creating my own patterns; I was too busy looking at yours.

I was also stuck in trying to heal my father, so I spent a lot of time trying to heal you rather than just loving you. From now on, may my presence alone be healing, and may we remember to see each other as healed instantly.

I forgive myself for taking so long to understand and let go of my patterns. May I now enter my real life which is complete and holy. May I always transcend any negative patterns that have kept me from perfection in relationships before.

I would love you all to come back so we could see and renew our relationship and heal each other.

Thank you for being my guru.

To all women I have loved greatly and who have loved me:

I have always felt you were there for me, and I trusted you more than men. I have had a need to spend all these years around men, trying to work it out. I was never trying to avoid you. I have always felt my relationships with you were good, and most of the snares have been caused when I set you up as my sibling. I have always learned a great deal from you.

I hope that any misunderstandings between us are cleared up by this letter; I hope it will be helpful to you. I appreciate your supporting me in becoming a leader and I support you as well in whatever you do. It helps to give up the thought that men don't like powerful women. I have found that men are often tired of the responsibilities that come with power and need a little rest. They really do like our help in cleaning up the world.

I hope you will join me in taking responsibility for getting our relationships the way we want them. I hope you will get turned on with me to the game of perfecting oneself.

Celebrate being a woman.

31

Personal Accounts from Graduates

Dear Sondra and Bobby,

I'm feeling a lot of gratitude for you both today and I want to share it with you. I am doing a lot of things now that I enjoy and though I won't see you at the advanced training next weekend, I want to send you my love and acknowledgments. You two have served me beautifully in the past year.

When I stumbled into a Sonny Stokes seminar last Sept. 9 in N.Y. and then into the LRT in October in N.Y., I was holding onto a marriage that was overloaded with sadness, a career as a book marketing manager that was finding me thinking more about my writing career, my psychology career and my self-healing than about my work, and in general feeling like my twenty-four years of excitement, new horizons, and accomplishments were about to slow down, become headed toward security and complacency, and find me more melancholy and restrained.

In very simple terms, LRT said to me "Hey, you don't have to give up your divinity. Growing up ain't growing old. Taking responsibility don't mean holding your breath to fight inflation."

The personas that you two had in that training in October were so different from any two people I had ever trusted, befriended, or been interested in. And yet I knew from the start that you were winners, that you were honest, and that you were examples of what it is like to grow and grow some more. I knew that your risk-taking, vulnerability, and tremendous energy were the things I had always valued in myself. I cried three boxes worth at that training, committed myself to move to San Diego, to a Ph.D. program in self-healing, and to an openness that I'd never permitted myself.

In San Diego, things were clicking for me beautifully. I established an outstanding friendship with Binnie, made more friends and associates than I'd ever known, spent every day at the beach learning from the gulls and the waves what I hadn't learned in Detroit, Pittsburgh, and New York, and loved the holistic psych courses that were helping me youth myself.

So I decided to give it a try and go to Santa Barbara in March. And that weekend, which still has over one hundred reels of outstanding film footage in my mind, was the source of so much of what is perfect in my life right now. The friendships, the business relationships, the sense of body mastery, the levels of relaxation and pleasure, all opened me up to new levels of commitment and satisfaction in my life. And with such little effort.

Right now things are very smooth and rich in my life. Even when one of my partners is screaming or I am putting myself way over my head in an investor or customer discussion, I feel all the rebirthing tools at my disposal, all the sources of letting go and being in the moment. I had been pursuing four different strains of myself for a number of years, feeling that they were separate, writer/businessman/healer/teacher, and now find that every day in my work setting up a new group, researching the projects, advising my partners, and making commitments to goals and visions that will have major impacts on the quality of life in the '80s, all four of my aspects are in use and in harmony.

I am grateful to both of you and to the LRT for being so instrumental in my path. I want to continue to give and receive with the LRT as I have. In addition to sharing all this, I want you to know that I am open to your ideas, suggestions, and loving energy.

And how is my primary relationship? I'm very happy with myself. Wednesday was my wedding anniversary and I had been to a homeopath/chiropractor in the morning. I was feeling very vulnerable and teary-eyed and went home and cried loud and long. I was releasing my pictures of my marriage, the ones that were not true. My wife and I are wonderful friends. We've filed a separation agreement and will have a N.Y. divorce one of these days. I've had some wonderful relationships since leaving N.Y. and will continue to find loving people who increase my aliveness. Now that I've cleared out a mass of sadness and holding on, I expect that a more complete primary relationship will emerge in my life.

Love,
Lenny

Dear Sondra,

Just for fun:

L	*R*	*T*
Learning	Right	Thinking
Loving	Readiness	Thought
Lasting	Righteousness	Training
Light	Revealing	Truth
Living	Rather	Today
Love	Remember	Truth
Lightness	Rightness	Togetherness
Luscious	Rushing	Tingles
Likeable	Redhot	Topics
Laughter	Radiance	Transcendence
Life	Redirected	Toward . . .
Limitless	Rainbows	Transmitted

Looking forward to seeing you next month. Our training is going to be out of sight!

Love,
Roger

The following was written by a very young girl, Esther, after her mother completed the LRT. She read it at a reunion of graduates shortly after her mother, Louise, had been in the Training.

Louise: Good morning Tuesday! I love you!
I love Esther.
I love being Esther's mommy.

Esther: I love being Louise's daughter!
I love Louise!!!!!!!
I love the world!

Louise: I love the world too. YEAH!!!

Esther: I love being alive!!!!!!!
I love going to school.

Louise: I like going to work.

Esther: I love iceskating!
I love rollerskating.
I love, love, *love* sports.
I feel very loved today.

Louise: I am very loved.

Esther: I love god.
I love learning about science.
I love happiness and peace.
I love being loved.
I love giving love to others.
I love the roar of the ocean.
I love silence.
I love playing backgammon.
I love the sound of the soft purring of a cat.
I love to go out to lunch!!!!
I love to look at fish.
I love physical fitness.
I love running.
I love relaxation.

I love all kinds of animals.
I love writing.
I love riding my bike.
I love nature.

Mom, I know that you can lose some weight! If you think "I'll lose some weight," it will become true.

Love, Essie

Dear Mom, Are you having a good time? The LRT changed your life! I'm glad that you and I are getting along well now! I hated the times when we were always arguing, didn't you? Have a nice day!

Love, Essie

32

Your Relationship with the LRT

I look forward eagerly to having each of you in the Training so that I can get to know you. Not only is the Training a wonderful place for you to clear all that is in the way of your receiving, and not only is it the place to create a totally new mental model for great relationships in the New Age, but also it is a great place to meet other aware people.

As I feel more and more complete, the Training is becoming more and more fun; in fact, it is turning into a great extravaganza. The Trainings have always been fun for me and the other trainers, and now the fun is accelerating. In the LRT people are even able to have fun while crying. I tell them never to miss an opportunity to cry, so people learn to enjoy their depressions and shorten them fast. We cry a lot and express a lot and laugh a lot, and everyone falls in love. Sometimes, when I finish the Training it is 2 A.M. because nobody wants to leave.

The LRT family represents the healed family. It becomes the family you always wanted. Then, when you take the time and the responsibility for cleaning up all your past relationships within your natural family, they become once more your chosen family and everything begins to look bright.

The LRT provides a place to work out your negative feelings safely, and it keeps you from projecting them onto those with whom you live. It is a place where there is enough energy, love, and support for you to let go of old negative mental mass effortlessly, because the energy of everyone in the room will push it out of you. After that you will get high together and have a good time. The only thing you have to give up is your misery. It might be hard to do that all alone out there, so we welcome you into the LRT family.

For information on the Loving Relationships Training nearest you and for information on rebirthing, contact:

LRT International
P.O. Box 1465
Washington, CT 06793
1-800-INTL-LRT
or
(203) 354-8509
FAX (203) 350-6735

PART THREE

Relationships with Immortalists

Relationships with Immortalists

What is it like to have a relationship between two Immortalists? First of all, let me say that life is totally different. There is a pervasive sense of continual well-being. There is a new feeling of safety and peace. There is less fear because the purpose is to constantly further each other's aliveness. There is plenty of time to handle everything that could come up. The relationship is *eternal*, immediately, and although the form of the relationship may change, many times, *leaving* no longer is an issue. There is an abundance of joy, happiness, and outright bliss. There is a natural telepathy that occurs when the two are apart. Since love is very pure without the projection of the death urge, more spontaneous healing happens in the aura and presence of an Immortalist. Two together provide miraculous energy. They support each other's continuing aliveness always; and this makes it safe to surrender totally. It is like a dream come true.

In the mortalist mentality, there is struggle, illness, pain and the result is death. This sadness of the tragic end to a relationship is overwhelming to the mate left behind. He often feels there is no choice but to die also, and often sees no point in going on "alone." A "deathist" is convinced that there is no way out except to die and has agreed that it is a short life, approximately 70 years. Death is "popular" about 70, and popular ways to kill oneself are to create cancer or heart disease or some similar catastrophe. A "deathist" believes that this is just the way it is and that there is no other alternative. For this, he often secretly hates God. Two deathists will tend to reinforce each other's belief systems and go to the grave together. They have become victims of a belief system handed down through the ages.

An Immortalist knows that this was not the way God intended to call His children home. An Immortalist knows that he can master his body if he masters his thoughts; and that he can continually raise the vibratory rate of his cells to increase his aliveness and youthfulness. He gets together with another Immortalist who helps him to do this. Together they form a holy relationship for the purposes of spreading light to the world. An Immortalist gravitates toward another who loves life, has positive thoughts and wonderful energy.

Prior to this decade, however, it was not safe to talk about such ideas, which seemed "outrageous." Immortalists more or less kept the "secret" to themselves in order not to be locked up, ridiculed, or stoned. (Most people would rather "defend their position" that death is inevitable than even consider looking at another possibility; people hate to be wrong.) Now, however, thanks to some brave souls like my good friends Bobby Birdsall and Leonard Orr, who had the guts to speak out on this subject publicly even before it started to become popular, things are changing. My relationships with these two men are things to marvel and my only regret is that I cannot write about the thrill of it all to my satisfaction. And of course, Babaji, the Immortal Master, is our teacher; as I complete this book, Leonard is again with him in the Himalayas.

I would like also to let you get a taste of some of my other relationships with Immortalists, especially the other Certified Rebirthers, who are like fellow disciples to me. How I met each one is like a miracle and being together with them are absolutely the highlights of my life. At this time we are all constantly traveling about teaching healing and love and Immortality and Rebirthing. I am very impressed with the work and contributions of each of my fellow Certified Rebirthers. I have always considered this honor to be like a "Rights of Passage" spiritually. We are all totally committed to each other and the healing of the planet. Probably one of the most important aspects of our relationships is the way we have created a "checks and balances" agreement in that, we could in fact "de-certify" someone who was not living up to the quality of what we expect spiritually. Therefore there is no casual commitment and no position of "tenure." We all have totally agreed to surrender to God, Rebirthing, Immortality, and the Truth and to each other and especially to the highest spiritual thought at any moment. Our mission is the same and the commitment is total. There is an everlasting bond that is beyond any petty upset or problem. It is a spiritual family of serving in the highest order.

33

Bobby

When my mother met Bobby Birdsall, the first thing she said was, "That man is a miracle."

When I met Bobby Birdsall, I hated him. My mother, who was my first trainer, of course, was obviously clearer and more intuitive about Bobby Birdsall. Not for long though. It took me about five minutes to see the truth. I realized that anyone who could stir up outright hate (which I almost never feel) in me had to be my ultimate guru. And so I went over to him and asked him if I could make him breakfast—this stranger, this little man who took over my housemeeting without even introducing himself, this man who told the truth so fast that it was painful to me. On some level, however, I knew that that was my own hate I was feeling in his presence. Something about his immense energy (immense love) blasted out of me some hate I would rather not have looked at. But apparently I was ready to look at it. I drew him in. And over breakfast, I surrendered to him as much as I could. But it took me over a year, maybe more than two years, to surrender all the way. I was afraid of him. He seemed wild and volatile and too smart. I was terrified he would get angry at me. I knew he could read my mind.

But then one day he certified me, this man I hardly knew

but who knew me so well. He said, "You are a little dizzy, but I don't think you have a negative thought in your head." I couldn't believe this man loved me so much and was giving me total approval. Another year went by, and we got a little closer in India, hanging out in strange places.

One day the center manager called me from New York and asked me if it was OK if Bobby Birdsall assisted with Rebirthing in the LRT, even though he had never taken the Training. This was against my policies; but I immediately said, "Yes," because in my eyes Bobby is an exception to everything. But then I became quite afraid. I was afraid of two things: Either Bobby would get mad and walk out of the LRT; or else he would take over the whole thing.

When I got to N.Y., Bobby was not there. He was late. His car had blown up on the way, which he immediately confessed to the group and claimed was due to the fact that he was resisting love. Even though he was late he got there just in time for *his* introduction. So he was the last one. He stood up and said, "I am here to cry," and then sat down and did just that. He surrendered to me totally, took the whole Training without leaving; and only took over when I asked him to telepathically. It was the only time in the history of an LRT the whole room went into a spontaneous Rebirth. I felt so safe with him in the room, I kept right on doing what I was doing (participating in the healing of a woman who was re-experiencing being an autistic child); I knew Bobby had the rest of the room covered even though they were all on the floor breathing. I did not have to turn my back once and leave the woman I was working with. It was one of the most outstanding Trainings up to that point. I guess it was then our real working relationship began. He came up to me after the Training and said, "I will follow you forever." I thought I was following him. (Now I follow him following me.)

During that training when Bobby was my "student," an interesting thing happened. While he was re-experiencing being an orphan, he got very sad and "stuck." I did not see him at first, all rolled up in the fetal position in his chair. But I did experience that the energy in the room was suddenly *jammed* totally and I could not think straight. At that moment a horn got stuck in a car outside in a parking lot. It was blaring and blaring. I turned to the group and said, "Somebody is really stuck in here," and my head turned right to Bobby. I told him he better stand up and share his feelings. As soon as he shared, the horn stopped. As soon as he sat down the horn got stuck again. So then I told him to stand up again and finish. As soon as he finished, the horn went off and stayed off. This is life with Bobby. (I have seen elevators slow down and stop between floors when there is an important lesson he has to give someone in the elevator. I have seen him drive around seven curves at night with his eyes closed. The funny part of that was I was never afraid at all. I would raise up my head and see he was sleeping, going around curves, and I would lie down and know I was just fine.)

Somewhere we went on the road together . . . we can't seem to remember when. It was only a few years ago, but it seems like a million years. One day was like a year when I was with Bobby. That was because we packed a year's worth of living into one day. Sometimes one sentence Bobby said saved me years.

One day I looked at Bobby, knowing we were in this together, and knowing that we had to get along 24 hours a day in all kinds of tough situations, and knowing that we were both extremely powerful, and knowing that I did not want this relationship to get messed up, and knowing it could blow up with all that energy unless I thought of *something* to handle it, and knowing that no matter what, our spiritual purpose came first and our spiritual connection came first, and knowing he knew all that, I *finally* said, "Bobby, I think we should play this game: In order to keep our relationship perfect and to keep it from ever blowing up, let's agree to a game where we each surrender to the highest spiritual thought at any moment. If you have it, I surrender and *get off it* . . . my former position. If I have the highest spiritual thought, *you* surrender and get off your position. We will easily feel the highest spiritual thought in our bodies. And in case we don't get who has the highest spiritual thought, we will go apart awhile and meditate."

He agreed *immediately* to my game, which filled me with wonder. He not only agreed, he "got it" totally and never asked me to repeat it or asked me a question about it. From then on we played it and played it well and we played it better and better per minute. Bobby liked to tell the world that the only arguments we ever had never lasted more than five minutes.

The only time Bobby ever screamed at me was when my mind was stuck. I tried to make sure he never had to scream at me very long or very often. The minute he started screaming, I realized my mind must have been stuck. Usually it happened when I was afraid to jump to a new level. He was always right.

What can you say when some one can read your mind so easily all the time? Sometimes when we came together after having been away from each other for a few days, he would walk up to me ever so gently and say, "Don't worry, I read your mind before you even got here." I just had to remain willing to be exposed, and constantly! I knew what I was doing when I allowed him so totally into my life. I would have quit my career or destroyed it long ago without him there to encourage and coax me. And the relationship was not one-sided because Bobby knew how I healed him also. And he knew I would also do anything to get him through something that was not working in his consciousness.

Whenever I started to get too serious or "heavy," Bobby was there immediately to crack me up with laughter. And any ailment I had seemed to clear up immediately when he was near. I found myself unable to hang on to negative states of consciousness for very long when I was with him. In other words, I had to be continually willing to "get off it," which I was, so there was not much problem.

At times however, my mind could not compute a friendship so deep, my mind could not compute this much love, especially since we were not sexual partners. (We always liked to say we turned each other *up*, not on.) We always seemed clear on our spiritual mission together and we were immediately like brother and sister. But in the old days, when we had little money and could only afford one hotel room on the road, we often slept in the same bed. We used to end up with our heads together and bodies apart like a pyramid. The energy was like a thousand lighting bolts together. We never could sleep at all because it was too much energy; so we would get up and take long walks around the city we were working in. Sometimes I looked at him and I thought he knew something about me that I didn't know. He acted like he saw my whole life ahead of me and he knew exactly how I was supposed to proceed.

I used to worry how another man in my life would handle all this. How would my primary relationship react to my relationship with Bobby? After all, it looked like I came complete with Bobby. It was a package. Then one day I realized that any man who wouldn't love Bobby as I did, I wouldn't want to be with anyway.

Bobby had always given his total heart to the man in my life. He had thrilled him, amazed him, praised him, healed him, processed him, and taught him everything. Even when he knew the man was not right for me, he would help me in it and support me. But if he ever saw me suffering too much or being upset too much, and if my work was being affected by that relationship, he might quietly take that man's picture off my bulletin board so I would wake up.

My friendship with Bobby certainly did not keep me from attracting other men. Nor did it hinder in any way my relationships with other men. It only added. I could sit down with him and have help at any moment to clear up any snags. It would be cleared well and quickly too, as long as we were willing to expose everything and surrender to the highest spiritual thought. I offered the same space to Bobby, of course, when he was with another woman.

We highly recommend that you too, have someone you can totally confide in besides your mate. Someone you love and trust and does not make you feel guilty.

My relationships look strange to some people because they

don't fit the traditional forms. There is a lot of change and I do experiment, frequently engaging in some very "off the wall" research. My main goal, however, has always been to master all forms of relationships without pain. I wanted to master the art of being married, living alone, living with someone else, having multiple relationships, and all other forms. I wanted to be able to teach how to create relationships painlessly, stay in one painlessly, and change one painlessly.

And I have learned well from Bobby: There are *no shoulds;* there are *no supposed tos.* You don't have to have relationships one way or another. You don't have to be married to be OK. Just because someone else is married or in a big relationship does not make them any better or you any worse. Just because your relationship changes, does not mean life does not work for you. *You always get what you need.* During some periods in your life you might need to be alone and that is the healthiest thing. There may be some periods in your life when you need to have many relationships to get many lessons. At another period in your life marriage might teach you the most. You will always set it up so you get the lessons that are important for you and you will naturally create situations that will heal you the fastest and get you to give up the ego. All kinds of different relationships are going on in the universe and they are all healing, and one form is no better than another.

The main thing to get clear on is your relationship with the *Universe.* When that one is working, all the others will, no matter what form you are in or not in!

34

Jim

When Jim Morningstar got certified, I did not know him very well. But I certified him because my intuition told me what I needed to know. I knew he was an excellent Rebirther and I knew he was totally committed. Psychically, I could see nothing that should stop him from having that honor. He is probably the first one I did on straight telepathy alone. And I was not wrong. This year in the annual Jubilee, he was brilliant in the way he kept pulling our group together. At times we begged him to be the chairperson and run the meetings. He seemed to be the one who could most keep us on purpose and keep the meetings in order.

Jim is presently the only certified Rebirther who is married and has children. This is a bonus for the rest of us because he adds balance to the group. While the rest of us are tripping around the country, he is more stable and operates out of the midwest (Milwaukee). This has been very helpful to the rest of us, because at least we know we can always find Jim. He has been totally willing to be in charge of Theta International, something the rest of us avoided and we appreciate him for this.

We do look to him to sort of "get us together," which is

often a very difficult task since our schedules change constantly and at very short notice.

I have always been fascinated by Jim's face which to me depicts incredible wisdom and the fact that he is a very old soul.

Recently when I stayed with Jim and his wife, Joan, I was blown away by the experiences I had there. The first night we literally stayed up all night discussing body mastery— learning to teleport, etc.— but mostly just loving each other and healing. I had the feeling that Jim would stay up with me ten more nights in a row if that was what I needed. Although I had never doubted the quality of his work or that he deserved to be certified, my constant traveling had kept me from getting to know him as much as the others.

One night, we all got in the tub. Bobby had been Rebirthing himself for hours. I had not had a wet rebirth by Jim before. He was so perfect that I began to cry softly and let go. This was a perfect short Rebirth; however in the next two days, an amazing thing happened. My breasts and hips began to grow some more. I was, quite simply, astounded. My hips had always been too flat from holding them in where I was hit at birth and from fear of being spanked again. While being rebirthed by Jim and Bobby, together, I must have felt safe enough to let go and released some hormones I had suppressed.

Relationships and the Body

My body is broadcasting, communicating the state of my love affair with myself twenty-four hours a day. If I'm on the "outs"—judging myself, punishing myself—my body vividly portrays this drama for the world to see. In an attempt to hide this display many folks try to vacate the premises, leave their body (perhaps for "higher spiritual planes") when they start to feel negative. The body is put on automatic pilot until the "heat is off," so to speak. This temporary vacation, however, is also a direct communication of where I am with myself— out to lunch!

Rebirthing reduces the base level of fear I carry with me in my body. I now feel safe enough to stick around when things get hot; in fact, I start to turn the heat into pleasure. The degree of pleasure I'm giving myself on a continual basis is my body's barometer for how much safety I have integrated and fear I have released. From this point of view, my body serves as a safety/fear meter and reacts to every thought I think. The degree to which I am in my body also reflects the degree to which I am willing to be aware of my base level of trust.

I observe that we all are intuitively aware not only of our body messages, but also of everyone else's. There is a difference, though, in how much each one of us is willing to let this intuitive sense into conscious awareness. I will tend to gravitate towards those who have a similar amount of basic safety in their life. They may choose to be continually pushing their limits or to be hanging back and letting others go first, but this is just a variation in style. It is their basic level of safety/love which attracts me; and it is their body which broadcasts this in the physical universe.

Those whom I have assumed to have more safety and mastery than I in the physical universe, I had always put on a pedestal. There they remained, distant and untouchable. When I started to admit and acknowledge the same level of trust in my body that I sensed they had, I took them off the pedestal and had a physical, bodily relation with them — hugged, had dinner together, etc. . . .

Within the various levels of safety are a number of variations in body type. These are like personality theme songs which I can retain even though I increase my level of safety. I generally take these themes less seriously and identify with them less the safer I become. The body types reflect my character and set the tone for the approach I have toward other bodies, that is, my relationships.

The first body type is called *fragmented*. Folks who are predominantly this type have participated in an early life experience of apparent coldness, rejection, or hostility, either prenatally or around the time of birth. The basic belief they adopt is that the world (and their body) is not a safe place to be. As a defense from this belief, they adopt a detached attitude, seeing themselves as a free spirit, for example, above material or mundane matters. Their bodies appear disjointed, like a collection of parts not quite all working together. There is a frozen appearance to their body, in particular a mask-like quality to the facial expression. Very little direct or warm eye contact is made. Their fear is that to be fully in their body, contacting another, will bring out their original feelings of terror and the rage they felt before choosing forgiveness. Thus, their first line of defense under stress is to leave, either remove their body entirely, or where this is not safe, leave psychically. The talent they develop is an extreme inner sensitivity to their world (if they cannot fight they must be continually on the alert to flee). This sensitivity is often turned into marvelous artistic and creative expression.

Their relationships are often intellectual or "spiritual." If the body gets involved, they tend to be mechanical (vacate) or take on another personality in order to be safe to feel. They relate through ideas, but communication about their real feelings is difficult. When there is danger of unpleasant feelings, they avoid or, all of a sudden and without explanation, are gone. They sense and are attracted to genuine warmth and safety, but they also know when you are angry at them and holding it back. What they are looking for in themselves and in their relationships is basic safety in feeling their body, expressing their emotions, and enjoying other bodies—food, clothes, sex, etc. When you can accept their level of fear, let them proceed at their pace, and be genuine yourself in relation with them, the door to their heart starts to open. They will then stay or keep coming back to accept the love on the other side of the early fears. When they are solidly in their bodies, their artistic and creative expression takes on a different quality and the richness of their sensitivity and expression is truly rewarding.

The second body type is the *oral*. The early life experience in which they participated (usually during their first year) was not that they were unwanted or hated, but rather that they were abandoned or there was not enough for them—deprivation. The basic belief is that they never get enough. Their countering or reactionary theme is that "If I love enough, I'll be loved," or just "I'm self-sufficient." Their body reflects this sense of deprivation with a collapsed chest area (even though women's breasts can be quite developed). Their pelvis tends to be locked forward and the knee joints locked back, giving the sense of effort in holding themselves up. They tend to locate themselves in their head (which is often thrust forward), especially the mouth region. They often take the sucker role—being a sucker for love which they pretend to lack. But when love or attention is given, it is never enough. Under stress the tendency is to collapse. The talent they develop is for learning what others want—empathy. Perhaps if they give others what they want, they will get what they want also.

In relationships, when they learn the art of receiving fully, they no longer feel like they need to suck the other dry or pretend they need no one. They often attract others with bursts of energy, brilliance, and self-sufficience. If, however, others are not there to support them through the "let-down" period or depression, resentment follows. Faith in their genuine ability to support themselves through the highs and lows which they experience is the best support you can give them. Do not buy the program that they or you have not done enough. As they release the fear of loss—which is really abandoning themselves when it looks like others are not around—their ability to empathize, give, and receive freely is a joy to experience.

The third body type is called *upward displacement.* The early life game (usually between the first and third years) is a power struggle over whose will is going to control their body—either their will or another's. If the parents, for example, feel the emerging will of the child is a threat to their authority and are good at overpowering or seducing the child to get their way, the child may choose to see all relationships as a contest over who will win. "To be on top of it" means to be above any feeling of weakness or helplessness. Their basic belief is that to admit to feeling is to be weak, since their feelings never seemed to make any difference in getting what they wanted from their parents. Their countering theme is "I'm in control."

Their body may display the "rising-above-the-situation" or overpowering style by being large and muscular on the top and relatively thin in the pelvis and legs. Or their body may display more even proportions but have a very alluring seductive quality especially in the eyes. Under stress they control and rise above or seductively manipulate to get their way. They often develop their leadership qualities to a high degree and have a talent for holding their ground and winning while others are running for cover. They think on a grand scale.

In relationships they can be very smooth, immediately likable. After knowing them awhile, however, you may realize that you do not really know them. They seldom reveal their hidden feelings and react very defensively when they fear being controlled. If you are able to hold your own self-esteem in the face of their threats and threatened feelings, you help them release their fears of having no strength. They begin to see that their strength and lovability is not dependent upon whether they get their way or not. They are then able to let down and have it be pleasurable rather than a defeat. They then can release the struggle for control and use their leadership abilities to lead toward pleasure in their relationship with themselves and those around them.

The fourth body type is the *withholding*. Here the game is shame— often an early experience of being humiliated for not holding in what the parents thought should be held in. The most obvious example of this occurs around toilet training (second to third year). The basic belief is that I am loved when I hold my shit in and ridiculed when I let it out inappropriately. Life is a struggle to hold in and "I must suffer and 'be good' to get what I want." Therefore, I am working all the time, and in the end "no one appreciates the job I've done for them." Their body portrays a stuffed and squashed image. The neck is thick, the trunk is usually larger with the waist short and squat. The tail bone is tucked under (like a dog with his tail tucked) and the ass is squeezed and often smaller than the rest of the trunk proportions. Under stress they tend to provoke and otherwise deal indirectly with their anger — whining, sarcasm, complaining. The talent they develop is endurance in their helping. They will stick with you and work through a project long after others would quit in frustration.

In relationships the withholder tends to harbor hurts and angers. They will do what you want but often feel underlying resentment if it is not what they want and then feel unappreciated for their efforts. "You don't know how much I've suffered for you." Beneath this heavy struggle is a creative spirit waiting to be joyfully released. The key is often to be willing to give and receive freely from them. Knowing that they no longer have to please you to be loved, and that sharing their anger directly is safe opens the way for their heart. They will try to get you to "work" as hard for their love as they do for yours. As you model it, so they will begin to appreciate the difference between working for love and allowing yourself to have it regardless of the messes you seem to have created. Beneath the protective layer, withholders have stored up a wealth of warmth and creative expression to be shared.

The fifth and last body type is the *rigid*. Disappointment is the early experience played out in their male/female relationships. Love and acceptance were forthcoming until the emergence of their sexuality (usually third to fifth years) and then they seemed to be held out by their opposite-sex parent. Their theme is "No one is going to hurt me again." Their belief is that "I am a loving person whom no one understands." Having a strong presexual basis for love and support, their bodies are usually well-proportioned, energetic, and lively. Their eyes are bright but there is a layer of armoring around their trunk; their back is rigid. They tend to be successful, personable and well-grounded in their bodies. Under stress they will blow off steam rather than hold it in. They have a talent for dealing effectively with the material world.

In relationships, however, there is a split between their loving and their sexuality. It seems to them that they can have one or the other but not both in the same lover. They are continually looking for success in love and meeting with disappointment when the intimacy brings out the hidden fear and hurt. In men this leads to the madonna/prostitute syndrome: "I love and admire my wife, but I can only have sex pleasurably with someone who is not like mama." In women this leads to hidden seductiveness, drawing men with the lower half of the body but holding their heart away with the upper, waiting for that knight on the white horse who will sweep them away and overpower their fears of complete closeness. Leaving the intimacy or causing their lover to leave keeps the game going. The uniting of love and sexuality starts with self-acceptance. This includes admitting and enjoying incestual feelings while releasing the judgments and anger around them. This allows relationships to be entered without hidden anger and fear building toward the expected disappointment. Then sexual or nonsexual contact is a conscious choice and can include a more full and satisfying union with the heart when so desired. The enthusiasm, vitality, and worldly competence they bring to a relationship is fulfilling on many levels.

As you might have experienced in reading this account, we all participate to some degree or another in each of the body types described. We do tend to have our favorite, however, which becomes so much a part of us that we often are the last to recognize it. Bringing our major themes to light, admitting, forgiving, and releasing them is what transforms our body from a seeming prison to a perfect vehicle for giving and receiving love — and, after all, what else are relationships for!

Jim Morningstar

35

Bob

I can't ever remember having a negative thought about Bob Mandell. When he stood up to be certified as a Rebirther, he was unanimously approved; that was only right. He is a wonderful Rebirther: He is nice, he is nice looking, he is clear, he is loving, he is soft, and he is all those things one would want in a spiritual leader.

Many times I have come roaring into his apartment in New York, where he lives with Mallie and her children, unannounced, with my suitcases strewn all over the place, with my energy flying about, and roaring like a pack of animals. I have always been accepted no matter what I was doing or thinking. In the old days Bob and Mallie would organize for me and get everyone together for the LRT in New York. Sometimes Bob would help me lead it and sometimes he would lead it himself or with Diane. And once when Bobby had to leave suddenly for another city ten minutes before the Training was to begin, I called Bob and asked him if he would replace Bobby. He put on his jacket and walked out in front of everyone and did a superb job as though he was the one that was supposed to do it all along.

Guilt: Separation Insurance

Guilt is the mafia of the mind. It is a protection plan you sell yourself to avoid anticipated punishment. You figure if you punish yourself first, then God, or people, will leave you alone. (This is why guilt is always accompanied by resentment.) Since your thoughts are creative, the result of this thinking is feeling alone, alienated, and separate. You think you're warding off attack, but what you're really denying is the experience of love, joy, and aliveness. If you get really successful at guilt, you'll transcend mere emotional self-sacrifice and do yourself real bodily harm. Guilt is the ultimate bummer which serves no positive function but can add to your miseries until you reach your limit. The final solution for a guilty person is death — redemption in his mind, but the logical outcome of a life of martyrdom and masochism in mine.

Guilt is the major obstacle to success in relationships. How can you let yourself receive unconditional love when you fear the consequences? How can you surrender to love when you fear loss? How can you give yourself what you most desire when deep down you feel unworthy? So you hold yourself back, hiding the parts of yourself you judge unworthy of love, hoping to fool your partner into loving you when you're not loving yourself. This can never work. Even if the love you're seeking is given to you, you will not be able to receive it because you will have armored yourself with the judgments you've made.

Fear of love and fear of loss are the same. This is why people are afraid to fall in love. If love is a fall, you might get hurt. You might give your power away to your partner, feel totally vulnerable, and then be abandoned by your "source of love." No wonder people shake and tremble in the presence of overwhelming love. (These people look the same as those feeling unbearable loss.) Some people won't even let themselves approach this experience, so great is their fear of loss. They'd prefer to feel alone, maybe having numerous flings but always making sure they leave before they are left.

People in love are not necessarily less guilty. Their fear of loss might be so great that they hold on to a relationship that

no longer serves them rather than feel the torment of separation anxiety. These people are more or less frozen in their relationships. They use their relationships to protect them from
their true feelings, hiding in their shelter from the storm.
These relationships are doomed to failure because they are
based on total resistance to experiencing fear and loss. Since
what you resist persists, protective relationships perpetuate
fear and loss.

Why are we so guilty? Why do we think that pleasure leads to
pain, love to loss and life to death? Why do we continually re-
enact the story of the Garden of Eden and what is the meaning
of the story? And how does the pain and separation we experience at birth affect our relationships? What really happened
in the Garden was that man, and woman, gave their power
away, denied their divinity, allowed themselves to think they
lacked something—how could you lack in paradise?—and
consequently were expelled from the Garden. They deserved
it! They forgot their divinity. That was original sin. Separation
from paradise was the result. You can't be in paradise when
you're experiencing not having it all. Separation is inevitable
when you think you need something in order to feel whole.

At birth, we are also expelled from paradise. In the womb,
we float in the lap of luxury, completely nourished and sus-
tained without effort. Then, we are delivered! In the process
the mother feels fear and pain which the child often blames
himself for. We are born guilty. It seems like our aliveness con-
tributes to the suffering of the one we most love. In my opinion, this "infant guilt syndrome" is equally as powerful as the
more publicized "parental disapproval syndrome," and sub-
verts relationships more than we realize. Imagine the consequences of believing that your being alive hurts your lovers!
This one thought can cause you to surpress your feelings, withhold your joy, and deny your divinity for the sake of others.
And if you really are in love with someone special, you might
even be willing to hurt yourself physically (and die) to protect
your partner from your aliveness. On a lesser scale, many people believe that self-sacrifice is a legitimate sign of devotion.

Another effect of birth on relationships is the "claustro-phobia/suffocation syndrome." In the womb you gradually grew until your mother's space could no longer contain and nourish you. Paradise suddenly became hell. You were boxed in and had to leave to survive. So, you chose out. Then the obstetrician got his hands on you, cut your umbilical cord, and your first breath was full of pain and panic. In relationships, we often relive this same emotional sequence. We move from the bliss of new love to a gradual feeling of constriction and claustrophobia. It often seems that paradise has become living hell and that we have to leave the relationship to continue our personal growth. The only alternative is to drive your partner to leave you. Often it becomes increasingly difficult to breathe around your lover and you will find yourself opening the window on cold winter nights so you can get enough air.

The result of all this is "The Great Double Bind" of most relationships, the feeling that you can't live with a person and can't survive without him. So the fear of love and the fear of loss are joined in holy matrimony with Father Guilt performing the ceremony, smiling as still another unsuspecting couple bites the dust.

The alternative to guilt is innocence. We all know the feeling of innocence when we look in a child's eyes. What many of us have forgotten is that we all contain that divine innocence—that pure loving playfulness, sometimes deeply buried beneath layers of hurt and protection. How to regain that lost innocence is the quest of all the children of God.

In a way it's ridiculous to refer to lost innocence since you can never lose what is eternally yours. Still, it is often necessary to transform your perception of yourself, and others, in order to experience life as it really is. Since guilt is a form of pain, examining the nature of pain can shed light on a solution to the problem of guilt. Pain, in fact, is the effort involved in holding on to negative beliefs. Some thoughts that contribute to guilt are: I don't deserve love; I hurt others; others hurt me; when someone leaves me, it hurts; love means suffering; God doesn't approve of my having fun. If you have such thoughts in your consciousness, the first thing to do is relax. Take a few breaths, let go of the tension in your body and watch your negative thoughts go by.

Realize that you do deserve love, and that no amount of hard work, struggle, suffering, or success will make you any more worthy of love than you are right now. Know that you are the source of both love and pain, and so is everyone else. In other words, you don't hurt others, nor do others hurt you. The cause of hurt lies within the one wounded, not in someone who happens to be present when the punishment occurs. And when someone you love leaves, you never lose anything of real value. Whenever you appear to lose something, it's only to make room for something better. And leaving, what is that anyway? Bodies are energy in motion. They are always coming and going, entering and exiting, turning and returning. Why take other people's movements personally? If I'm with someone I love and I go away, what will determine her response is not my movement but her feelings about herself. If she loves herself, she will love me even as I leave. If she hates herself, she will resent my leaving. She might think she needs me around to feel love. This is that good old double bind: If she believes she needs me, she will hate both herself and me if I stay. She'll hate herself for being dependent and hate me for supporting her habit. She'll probably end up doing everything she can to drive me away. How ridiculous it all is! She is the source of her life, not me, and men will keep leaving her until she learns that lesson. The universe is that generous. Really, we should thank the lovers who leave us, thank them for the gifts they've given us and thank them for teaching us that we don't need them to feel love.

Of course, if you're stuck in feelings of neediness, helplessness, and dependency, you should honor those feelings, not avoid them. Remember, what you resist persists and what you accept dissolves. So do yourself a favor and be gentle, patient, and loving with yourself when you have these child-like feelings.

Forgive yourself. Forgiving is erasing your mind and opening your heart. Forgive yourself for thinking you don't deserve love by erasing all the good reasons—excuses—you've used to keep love out. Just change your mind. And forgive yourself for ever thinking you hurt someone or they you. Most of all, forgive anyone you're now resenting, from your parents to ex-lovers to old friends. Continued resentment will only add to your guilt since we usually hate ourselves for hating others.

A note on resentment! Resentment is a decision we made with our minds and hold with our bodies that we were betrayed, when, in fact, we betrayed ourselves. Sometimes it is beneficial to approve of yourself for resenting and blaming, to give yourself the space to do it freely. As long as you take responsibility for what you're feeling, any emotion—even blame—can be released and harmony can be restored. To blame without guilt is often the first step in forgiveness! An emotion is energy in motion propelled by a thought. The important thing is to allow your energy, which after all is your healing life force, to flow without obstruction. Think of all the times in your life you've held yourself back from feeling and/or expressing your feelings. Often, you'll end up resenting the person you're withholding from, blaming him for your lack of safety. This is called the "withhold, withdraw, resent syndrome," and the simple solution is to give yourself permission to feel and express all your feelings. *All feelings if fully felt will lead to the feeling of love!*

If your destination is innocence and your vehicle is forgiveness, your path might still be an emotional roller coaster until all your emotions are okay with you. Think of your feelings as your gurus, teaching you to love yourself unconditionally, even in the presence of fear, anger, and sadness. Love is, finally, a happy, life-supporting energy that flows through you when you flow through it. So don't give up. Persist! And know, even when confusion and hopelessness rear their twisted heads, you were born innocent and you remain innocent, and that anything else is a lie. Deep down in your heart you have always known this. And the more you surrender to your heart, the more you will celebrate the divinity of your essence.

Bob Mandell

Phil*

I really got close to Phil Laut when I was about to open the LRT in New York. The city excited me so much that I could not sleep at all. The night before the Training, wondering how I was going to do a seminar without having had any sleep for four nights, I sat and talked with Phil. Instead of thinking I was silly, he was so understanding and loving that he instantly relaxed me by saying, "Just tell them you are giving up sleep." He covered my next fear without me having to verbalize it, "And if you fall off the stool, so what?" Since Rebirthing it was true that I needed less sleep. I was no longer trying to suppress anything and therefore was not tired. But I was afraid to tell anyone for fear they would think I was weird. Phil totally accepted it, and I did the whole Training without any sleep. Phil always knew the thing to say that I needed to hear, and it was a joy to have him with me.

I regret that there is not space or time to write about Bill Chappelle (who is pure delight) and about all the other certified Rebirthers and immortal friends (two who have helped a lot are Diane Hinterman and Terry Cole Whittaker). I want to acknowledge them all for the contribution they have made to my life. And I definitely look forward to meeting all the new friends who will be coming into my life. I hope you are one of them.

*See Phil Laut's remarks on money in Chapter 14, p. 52

Fred

To me, Fred has always been everything I needed him to be. He represents the state of excellence. He has been endlessly thoughtful— a quiet Master who has been my personal guru, traveling companion, best friend, colleague, co-trainer, all-around teacher, all-around student, spiritual counselor, personal rebirther, rebirthee, client, therapist, consultant, advisor, and even entertainer through his fine, high-quality music. Fred has played a perfect three-hour classical guitar concert for me and my date on a houseboat; he has even serenaded me outside my bedroom door in a fabulous baritone voice, singing in many languages which he can also speak fluently. He has also performed perfect Tai Chi any time I have asked, putting me in supreme meditational states.

One day at the Jubilee I asked some people at the pool what they thought about Fred. Ellen said "He sparkles!" Suzanna said "He is brilliant and has very good taste in friends." Bob Mandel said "He is a Renaissance Man, a master of understated showmanship, a master of the Tai Chi of communication, a master of metaphysical diplomacy. People blossom in his presence. He is the 'catch of the day.'" Vincent reminded me how Fred had played cello for him the first hour they had met. "He is always pulling out a new talent," Vincent remarked. "He is a miracle of beauty, intelligence, expression, music and manners."

The way I met Fred was amazing in itself. I was out under the stars at Campbell Hot Springs soaking in the middle of the night. I had been rebirthing myself, and the last thing I expected was to see two nice-looking businessmen, dressed in suits, arriving at the springs (which were nestled in the woods and not that easy to find in the night). They came over the hill and approached me. When I shook their hand in greeting, sparks flew that were visible to all of us. With that I got out, grabbed a towel, and said "We'd better go have a talk." We went to the inn and began discussing all the healers we knew on the planet, and how we could get everyone to work together for the improvement of the planet.

That was my first meeting with Fred. It seemed as though we had known each other for eons. We have been working together ever since. I recall many trainings I have taught with Fred, where situations came up that seemed impossible. Fred always knew how to handle these situations immediately. He has always encouraged me to be a leader in my own right and gently pushed me to be all that I could be.

As well as I know him, and as deep as our spiritual relationship is, I have yet to understand the mystery of Fred. Many times I have felt that he is not understandable. Long ago I stopped trying to figure him out. Instead, I try to focus on the gratitude I have for the contribution he has continued to make.

I remember one night when my colleagues and I were invited to a very special dining experience. Fred decided he would introduce us to this master of the cuisine and he spent an hour preparing us mentally for this man who had cultivated perfection in dining. Fred's introduction of him was more perfect in itself that we could ever have imagined.

Immortal Relationships

How does the Immortal Relationship begin? It starts with the Moment of Recognition. Two Beings acknowledge each other as being. In that instant, each sees the other as complete and beautiful. The gesture is made through a meeting of the eyes, or sometimes by physical touch or by word. Treasure this moment; do not forget it.

The Immortal Relationship is complete at the outset, and its Essence never dies, although its form may change forever. This Essence is unique for each Relationship. Nothing can ever dilute or corrupt it. It can only be lost when one forgets or denies its existence. Do not deprive yourself of this love.

Out of the acknowledgment of Recognition and Completeness, there need be no pressure related to time. The creating of a form for the Relationship is by choice and is a process of giving and receiving pleasure. Because the Relationship is complete, there is no need. Because it is incorruptible, there is no jealousy. Need and jealousy are replaced by Peace.

The Immortal Relationship will be real for you to the extent that you can let go of two fundamental lies about your existence which you may have accepted at birth: first, that love comes from outside of you; second, that you need love to survive. What is really true is this: *you are love,* and *nothing can kill you.*

The Immortal Relationship is also the foundation of communication through art. Through what I have written you can recognize me.

I offer you this meditation so that you can begin to see what has always been true. All your relationships are Immortal.

Fred Lehrman

Diane

Once there was a beautiful Maiden
Who saw everything
felt everything
and knew everything.
But she was afraid to show it

SHE MASTERED EVERYTHING QUICKLY!

She was a Saint
And all her friends knew it
But she was afraid to show it . . .

Pretty soon she could no longer hide!
And God asked her to show it!

Diane is. Diane lives.
She is a gift in my life
I'd love to share with you.

PART FOUR

Appendix

A

Rebirthing Explained*

The purpose of rebirthing is to remember and re-experience one's birth; to relive physiologically, psychologically, and spiritually the moment of one's first breath and release the trauma of it. The process begins the transformation of the subconscious impression of birth from one of primal pain to one of pleasure. The effects on life are immediate. Negative energy patterns held in the mind and body start to dissolve. "Youthing" replaces aging and life becomes more fun. It is learning how to fill the physical body with divine energy on a practical daily basis.

The Birth Trauma
At the moment of birth, you formed impressions about the world which you have carried all your life; these impressions control you from a subconscious level. Many of them are negative:

> Life is a struggle.
> The universe is a hostile place.
> The universe is against me.
> I can't get what I need.
> People hurt me.
> There must be something wrong with me.
> Life is painful.
> Love is dangerous.
> I am not wanted.
> I can't get enough love.

Your impressions are negative because your parents and others who

*Excerpted from *Rebirthing in the New Age* by Leonard Orr and Sondra Ray. Millbrae, CA: Celestial Arts, 1977.

cared for you didn't know what you needed when you were born, and gave you a lot of things you didn't need: Lights that were too bright for your sensitive eyes, sounds that were too harsh for your ears, and touches of hands and fabrics too rough for your delicate skin. Some of you, despite the fact that your spines had been curled up for several months, were jerked upside down by your heels and beaten, which produced excruciating pain. Breathing became associated with pain and your breathing has been too shallow ever since.

But the physical pain is nothing compared to the psychic pain of birth. Nature provided that as a newborn you could receive oxygen through the umbilical cord while learning to breathe in the atmosphere (which was a totally new experience after having been in water), but the custom has been to cut the cord immediately, throwing you into a panic where you felt you were surely going to die right at birth.

Another significant psychic pain occurred when you were snatched away from your mother and stuck in a little box in the nursery. Most people never recover from this mishandling of the separation of mother and child. For nine months you knew nothing but the inside of your mother's womb. It was warm and comfortable until it got too small for you. What you needed was to be shown that the world outside is a far more interesting place, with a lot more possibilities than the womb, and that it could be just as comfortable, safe, and pleasurable as the place you had been. However, since your leaving that place was so traumatic, you have probably spent your entire life trying to get back there, never noticing or experiencing the full extent of the possibilities out here.

Fortunately, there are now some changes being made in the birth process. Frederic LeBoyer, a French obstetrician, delivers babies in dim light, with few sounds. He places each child on the mother's stomach, holding him gently, and waiting for the child to learn to breathe on his own. He cuts the umbilical cord only after it stops pulsating, and holds the child gently in a tub of warm water to show that there are comfortable and pleasurable experiences available outside the womb. The warm water immersion recreates the feelings of being in the womb. In the tub of water the muscles relax, the baby experiments with movement, a smile may appear. Several doctors in this country have adopted this method, and they say that "LeBoyer babies" are more relaxed, cry little or not at all, and seem to expect love and pleasure from their universe. They are brighter, less afraid, and almost never sick.

At the same time as Dr. LeBoyer was developing his process in France, Leonard Orr in California was discovering a way of helping a person at any age to get in touch with his birth trauma and remove it from consciousness.

The process Leonard created is very simple and yet extremely powerful. In the beginning, all rebirths were done in a hot tub. The rebirthee entered the tub with a snorkel and noseplug and floated face down while the rebirther and the assistant gently held him in place. The water proved a powerful stimulus in triggering the experience of being in the womb and being forced out of it. In fact, as the process evolved, it became clear that going in the water for the first rebirth was so powerful that it was too scary for some people. To avoid overwhelming them, Leonard devised the dry rebirth. He had noticed that it is the breathing and relaxing in the presence of a rebirther that is crucial to the success of the rebirth, and not the water, as he'd thought originally. The process works best when a person is dry-rebirthed until he has a breathing release, and then moves into wet rebirths.

Rebirthing occurs when people feel they are in an environment safe enough to re-experience their birth. Being in the presence of a rebirther — someone who has already worked out his or her own birth trauma — gives the rebirthee the certainty that "I will come out OK." The message is communicated, telepathically and emotionally, to the subconscious mind of the rebirthee; in addition, the rebirther will verbally encourage him by a gentle reminder that he survived his own birth the first time, and can do it again.

The rebirthing experience varies from person to person. As each discovers his negative conditioning, the rebirther assists in the process of rewriting the script by using affirmations. These are written to contradict specifically the negative decisions the person made at birth. So we create the view that:

> The universe and my body exist for my physical and mental pleasure.
> I can get all the love I deserve.
> I am glad I was born; I have the right to be here.
> I am safe, protected by Infinite Intelligence and Infinite Love.

Needless to say, when a person begins to adopt this view of the world his life changes drastically. So, for all of you who have ever dreamed of being reborn and starting life all over again, you can now make it possible!

Rebirthings generally continue until the rebirthee completes the breathing release and erases the negative mental mass which has grown out of personal laws formed at birth. After that, one can Rebirth oneself.

Any negative thought will inhibit the breath, but the most destructive, inhibiting thoughts are negative ones about the breath itself. Therefore, the negative thoughts you had about life itself while taking your first breath are the most damaging to your breathing mechanism. Reliving your first breath is one of the focal points of rebirthing and is one reason why we continue to call this spiritual, mental, and physical experience *rebirthing*.

After the rebirthing is completed, the merging of inner and outer breath and its rejuvenating effect becomes spontaneous and effortless. That is, breathing fully and freely with the spirit, mind, and body becomes the natural way for the individual consciousness to function. When rebirthing is completed in an individual, and the power of the breath is restored, spiritual enlightenment, the affirmations principle, and other spiritual techniques or philosophies (like Yoga or physical immortality) become all the more important because of the significant personality changes. Rebirthing cuts away human trauma at such a fundamental level that the people who complete it are transformed from working on themselves to playing in the universe. All self-improvement games become recreation and leisure activities which enlighten, rather than serious business. Rebirthing puts fun into self-improvement as well as into life itself.

The Breathing Release

Rebirthing is merging the inner and outer breath to experience the fullness of divine energy in the physical body. Re-experiencing birth is only necessary as long as it is inhibiting the breathing mechanism; so we have stuck with the term rebirthing and applied it to physical birth because the basic inhibition on the breathing mechanism was implanted on the individual consciousness during the first breath. It is also called rebirthing because in each session the divine infant is born again in human flesh.

The breathing release is the most important aspect of rebirthing. It is a critical release of all your resistance to life. The breathing release happens when you feel safe enough to re-live the moment of your first breath. It is physiologically, psychologically, and spiritually reliving the moment when you started to breathe for the first time. The breath mechanism is freed and transformed so that, from that moment on, a person knows when his breathing is inhibited and is able to correct it. This experience breaks the power of the birth trauma over the mind and body. A portion of the breathing release probably takes place in all genuine rebirth experiences, but the climax occurs when vibrating energy goes through the throat, usually causing constriction and choking just as on amniotic fluids when you took your first breath. This is the scariest part of rebirthing because the person goes through the first moment of his life when he struggled to breathe while drowning, suffocating and strangling in an attempt to get amniotic fluid out of the breathing passages and air in. That closeness to death must be cleared away before a person is safe. It is getting a person through this moment that is the art and primary role of rebirthing.

The breathing release puts the power of your life-force into your thoughts. Therefore, be careful what you think about when you are breathing! The danger of having the full power of aliveness without the wisdom of awareness is that you may destroy yourself more efficiently. We have noticed, however, that people who are destructive usually don't get rebirthed. If they try, they usually are unable to "let go" until they give up destructive thoughts.

Hyperventilation

Hyperventilation is the breathing release in process. Hyperventilation (medically described as breathing so deeply that there is a dramatic loss of carbon dioxide in the blood) is usually treated as a disease. It is actually the cure for subventilation. Subventilation is inhibited breathing, commonly called *normal* breathing. Hyperventilation is impossible for a person who breathes uninhibitedly.

It is important to discuss hyperventilation because many people think that it is something to fear and make the rebirthing experience more difficult for themselves than is necessary. One doctor who was particularly afraid of hyperventilating set the all-time record of five hours for a rebirthing by resisting it all the way through. Several hundred other doctors relaxed and went through it without difficulty.

What is called "hyperventilation syndrome" is a natural part of rebirthing. After rebirthing over ten thousand people, we have evolved a new theory of hyperventilation which is unanimously accepted by medical people who have completed their rebirthing. The new theory is that hyperventilation is a cure for subventilation. The birth trauma inhibits a person's breathing mechanism, causing shallow breathing. When a person breathes normally, fully and freely for the first time, without fear, it automatically produces some changes in the body. After watching ten thousand people successfully make it through a hyperventilation experience, we have concluded that all the person requires is calmness, safety, and encouragement to complete the process. If the person is encouraged to be patient, to breathe naturally and to relax while experiencing his fears, no harmful effects occur. On the other hand, if this natural process is interrupted by either the fear of the participant or the observers, the result seems to be perpetual fear of hyperventilation and its accompanying symptoms.

Our research has made the the old theory obsolete. We are not medical researchers, but we have been told by several doctors that one theory about the cause of hyperventilation is that it is caused by rapid breathing. We have found in all ten thousand cases that the rapid breathing cleared up the hyperventilation syndrome — including tetany and other accompanying characteristics — rather than caused it. We may not have the sophisticated technical machinery that the medical profession has, but since we have cleared up over ten thousand cases of the hyperventilation syndrome with rapid breathing, our theory deserves respect. The theory is that rapid breathing may accompany hyperventilation syndrome, but it is more a cure than a cause.

We have found that if a person has a voluntary rebirthing experience once a week until completion, it produces a feeling of profound health and well-being. After a person has relived the moment of the first breath, then hyperventilation syndrome no longer occurs. A person can breathe as fast and as hard as is physically possible without any undesirable effects. Therefore, our conclusion is that hyperventilation is a natural cure and not an illness.

In our work we learned that breathing fast was not necessary to induce the hyperventilation syndrome; we observed that relaxing in the presence of the rebirther produces the syndrome regardless of the breathing speed. Increasing the breathing speed, as long as the breathing is relaxed, eliminates the elements of the syndrome completely. We apologize to the medical profession if we are doing their work for them, but it was an accidental discovery on our part and we are willing for them to benefit from the research.

After observing over ten thousand cases, we concluded that although some physiological (chemical) explanations have some value, none of them fit all cases. We concluded that the only common denominator is fear and that all physiological processes seem to be controlled by psychological causes. Leonard defines fear as the effort involved in clinging to a negative thought which negates a substantive quality of Infinite Being. Any anti-life thought can cause what is called tetany in medical terminology. Rebirthees usually call this phenomena cramps, paralysis, or the "creeping crud." The phenomena doesn't occur with rebirthees who relax into the "tingling" energy sensation, who stay with a constant breathing rhythm, and who allow themselves to feel their fears. People who try to stop the energy and protect themselves get paralyzed. The cramps may be repeated for a few rebirthing sessions until the negative emotion can be verbalized and released. Then the individual can permit the tingling and vibrating energy to flow freely and evenly throughout the whole body. When the energy flows evenly and freely in the body, it heals, balances and grounds the person. The rebirthee feels a profound sense of peace, serenity and physical well-being.

This state seems to be permanent. Individuals who pursue rebirthing to this point report that simple breathing power is a whole new source of health, energy and pleasure.

The Energy Release

At some point in rebirthing there is a reconnection to Divine Energy and as a result you may experience vibrating and tingling in your body. It starts in different places in different people and, before rebirthing is complete, 'it usually is felt throughout the whole body. This energy reconnects your body to the universal energy by vibrating out tension which is the manifestation of negative mental mass. Negative mental mass can be permanently dissolved by continuing to breathe in a regular rhythm while your body is vibrating and tingling—experiencing your reconnection to the Divine Energy.

Major points of the energy release include the following:

1. Relaxation causes inner and outer breath to merge and the breath opens.

2. When the breath opens, the merging of the inhale with the exhale brings about the experience of Infinite Being on the physical level.

3. This breathing cycle cleanses the mind and body; there isn't necessarily any tingling or vibrating with this cleansing process.

4. If there is resistance or fear, then the body will tingle and vibrate. The vibration is not the energy but resistance to the energy. However, vibration is the cleansing process and should be welcomed. Resistance is negative thought previously impressed on the mind and body. At the completion of a breathing cycle resistance is dissolved and the person is breathing faster and there is no tingling. Understanding this is helpful for people being rebirthed the first time, otherwise they will have no way of knowing that rapid breathing eliminates the tingling. The assumption most have is that rapid breathing *causes* the tingling.

5. The truth is that rapid breathing is dissolving and pumping out tension and negative thought from the body and vibrating is incidental to the cleansing process.

6. After the cleansing, Divine Energy is coming in with every breath. There is no sensation, but the increase in vitality and health is evident in the body and one experiences bliss in the mind.

7. The energy release is actually dissolving resistance to Divine Energy.

The energy release in the body is so dramatic that many people are afraid of the vibrating sensations and try to stop them. Since the energy is your own life-force, you should not try to stop it. When you try to stop your own energy moving in your own body, it causes tightness, cramping, or temporary paralysis. Consider what your mind might go through at this point: The body is reconnected to the pleasure it felt when it was in the womb. The last time you experienced that much pleasure it led to your birth and the resulting trauma. Therefore, you believe that something terrible will happen again. This is where the pleasure precedes pain philosophy started; that is, the bliss and pleasure of the womb led to the pain of the birth trauma. So the pleasure being experienced through the vibrations creates a fear of the "inevitable" (which never happens). In experiencing a pleasure for the first time, we concern our minds with how we will eventually have to pay for the enjoyment, to the detriment of the pleasure. Therefore, you might try to suppress the vibrations to reject the sensation of your own life-force. If you try to stop these vibrations, however, a painful conflict will occur and you can paralyze yourself temporarily. *Paralysis is caused by resisting yourself.*

One part of your mind says, "I want to do this," and another part says, "Hold it, maybe I don't want to do this." This conflict results in paralysis in the body. It is the same conflict we had at birth. "I want to get out of the womb" and "I don't want to leave." The fear of irreparable damage is the idea that "If I go out of the womb, I'll never get back in." This fear of irreversible change is the origin of all fear. (This is also the basis for the fear of death.)

The paralysis usually lasts only for about ten or fifteen minutes although the fear is that it will be permanent and that it will cause irreparable damage. When it is over, you might think that the energy caused the paralysis. But it was *not* the energy that caused the paralysis! It is fear and resistance to the energy that caused the paralysis. However, if you believe in your mind that the vibrations, which were actually pleasurable, caused the pain, then you might keep resisting. When you felt pleasure and were afraid something terrible would happen, and something terrible did happen, you might conclude that you were right to try to stop it. You might think that, if you hadn't stopped that energy, something even worse might have happened. So the tendency is to keep resisting, and it gets worse. And each time it gets worse, you probably would conclude you did the right thing. You might want to say to yourself, "If it got worse when I tried to stop it, what would have happened if I hadn't tried to stop it?"

Not everyone goes through this erroneous reasoning process, but the people who do continue to close down and go into fear until the pain becomes excruciating. When it reaches that point, they finally start to let go and follow the instructions of the rebirther. As they breathe more efficiently, the paralysis immediately lessens. However, as the paralysis releases, the vibrating or tingling resumes dramatically. This usually frightens them and they close down again. Some people experience many such cycles until they can relax and breathe at a rhythmical speed. You can avoid all this if you will only let go to the experience of feeling your own life-force in your body.

Rhythmical breathing is pulling on the inhale and relaxing on the exhale in a continuous stream so that the inhale is connected to the exhale. The key is to relax into the tingling.

Rhythmical breathing empties the negative mental mass out of your body and enables you to incorporate the life energy into your body instead. If during the energy release you are willing to trust the instructions of the rebirther, in regard to your breathing, you can move through the energy release with a minimal amount of discomfort. Unfortunately, since the birth trauma is the original source of distrust, you might at this point enter into a period of distrusting of the rebirther and nothing that the rebirther does or says will seem correct. You may continue in the pain and if you are in pain you will blame the rebirther for the pain that you are causing yourself.

A negative thought stored in your body automatically resists the aliveness of Infinite Being. The presence of the rebirther automatically lowers the resistance; the rebirther can help alleviate your pain. Cooperation is the best thing you can do for yourself. Your birth trauma is "failing" at birthing yourself and so you might flunk rebirthing the first few times. Completion is when you become a good rebirthee and do it right.

People who become temporarily paralyzed in rebirthing may be more fortunate than people who don't, because they learn two things: One, as soon as they get in touch with their fear of the symptoms and let go of that fear, the paralysis ceases and their body opens and feels pleasure; they learn that behind all pain and fear is pleasure which is God's love. Two, if they don't get in touch with the fear and verbalize it but relax into the symptoms and keep breathing, the paralysis goes away anyway. So they learn that healing is inevitable whether they understand or not!

Therefore rebirthing is a model for all healing. The elements are as follows: Relax into the symptom so that you can get its message about your mind. Don't be afraid of it. Pain and fear are the effort involved in clinging to a negative thought. Behind all fear and pain is pleasure, which is the physical manifestation of the metaphysical love of God. All pain, all fear and all illness is resisting the pleasure of God's love and wisdom on some level.

Pleasure is natural. All else is unnatural . . . and ultimately self-destructive. If you don't relax into the pain and go through it to the pleasure that is behind it, life will become too much of an effort and you will love death more than life. *Death is loving pain more than you love pleasure.*

For people who don't experience the temporary paralysis, we can only assume they have mastered the pleasure-pain principle previously through some other means or that they may go through it in the future. The few people who are able to go through the rebirth experience without paralysis also have the ability to let go completely. The ability to let go during the energy release is based on trust.

The energy release gives you a new body. You feel connected to your body in a wonderful way—sensually—abundant physical energy and a sense of safety and serenity spreads over you. When the rebirthing experience is complete, this serenity becomes permanent. The primary thing that could interrupt it is the negative mental attitudes of others in your environment.

During rebirthing you need to trust that in the universe there is no natural force that will hurt you. Trust that it is your own mind which creates what happens in your body, and that you can uncreate it. Trust that the vibration is good energy that will heal you and mobilize the tension and negative mental mass, enabling you to breathe it out. Trust that the tingling and vibrating is "God loving you at a cellular level." Trust that the energy sweeping through your body is restoring your primal ability to experience pleasure and serenity. Trust your rebirther who has taken hundreds of people through the experience and every one survived. If you survived your birth, you will survive your rebirth!

Pictures

During rebirthing, possibly even the first time, you can achieve total recall of your birth scene. But you may become so preoccupied with your physical body that you will care very little about memories and pictures. However, the pictures usually become more and more obvious with each subsequent rebirthing session and after you have worked out the physiological stuff, you can sit down quietly at any time and recall events surrounding your birth. In other words, after the trauma has been removed, you will have the tendency to gain full memory of your birth experience and the events surrounding it. I have rebirthed several people who were adopted and had no conscious recall of their natural parents prior to that day. In their rebirth experiences, they were literally able to "see" their natural mothers and fathers and give me incredible details about their lives, which enabled them to understand and forgive the parents for having given them up for adoption. Hundreds of other people have remembered details they were never told. These details were then related to their parents, checked out and confirmed, to the amazement of the parents.

The main reason some people have trouble remembering their birth is the negative mental mass inhibits them from remembering anything before age three to five. Memory blocks caused by past traumatic experiences are a common subject of psychology. The theory is that painful experiences are blocked from the memory because the person does not want to remember the pain. Our theory is that remembering the experience releases the pain and frees the mind and body; and that the release is not painful, but sometimes intensely pleasurable. The fear of painful memories holds the pain in the mind or body to be experienced as pain or tension. To free your memory you have to get rid of the concept that remembering painful incidents makes the pain worse; and you have to get into the idea that the release is worth the time—and wonderful.

Rebirthing is focused on releasing rather than re-experiencing the trauma. Most people, when taking out their household garbage, don't find it necessary to examine each individual can, bottle, wrapper, and box before discarding it. However, it is a curious phenomenon that those same people, before letting go of any "psychological garbage," will find it necessary to meticulously pick through, sift, taste, touch, smell, analyze, classify, examine, and understand each item in order to make sure they don't throw out anything valuable. Using this analogy, we say that if psychoanalysis and psychotherapy are like diligently picking through your psychological garbage in an attempt to understand it, then rebirthing (in most cases) is like carrying out your garbage in one fell swoop. In the beginning some people find this very disconcerting, because the rebirthing process releases negative mental mass so quickly you don't have time to think about or understand it. After the rebirth, however, most people are so high and feel so good that they could not care less about "understanding" it.

Symptoms

We think of rebirthing as the ultimate healing experience because your breath, together with the quality of your thoughts, can heal anything. We have seen symptoms, from migraine headaches to sore ankles, disappear as a result of rebirthing. Respiratory illnesses, stomach and back pains have disappeared. Frigidity, hemorrhoids, insomnia, diabetes, epilepsy, cancer, arthritis and all kinds of manifestations have been eliminated. These illnesses seem to be caused or prolonged by the birth trauma. People get stuck in birth trauma symptoms and develop medical belief systems about them. Doctors then become mother-substitutes to support an infancy act. In rebirthing, we see people go through physiological changes in ten minutes that other people stay stuck in for years and from which they may die.

On the other hand, rebirthing creates a safe environment in your mind and body for symptoms from the past (example: childhood illnesses and patterns) to act themselves out. It is well to keep in mind that these symptoms are temporary and relatively easy to eliminate with the powerful ally of uninhibited breathing. But if in your mind you are afraid of these symptoms or resent them, you may inhibit your natural healing powers. Some of these symptoms can be bothersome and frightening. It is well to use physicians that you can trust, as well as spiritual and mental healers, to make it easier for you to get out of the traps in your own mind. Rebirthing is not for people who retreat from life in fear, who desire to curl up and die, unless they want to break up this pattern. Rebirthing is for people who are dedicated to aliveness and who desire to live fully, freely and healthily in spirit, mind and body.

We want to make it clear that the birth trauma is not responsible for everything. In a sense, the birth trauma is highly overrated, even though it is often responsible for terminal illnesses and many common maladies that plague people for life, including crippling of the breathing mechanism which may be the result most damaging to human happiness. When rebirthing clears these things up, the damage done by the birth trauma seems irrelevant. It is amazing that when you have a problem, it predominates and pervades everything; but when it is gone, it is impossible to remember what a burden it was. So the birth trauma pervades everything and dominates us until we are free and then we wonder why we made such a big deal of it. This paradox is a tragedy for gratitude, but a benefit to bliss and accomplishment. It is good to be grateful, but sooner or later we have to go on to the process of living. The first step is to let the birth trauma out of its suppressed prison in the individual's subconscious, second, to do the work of healing its damage to the individual's mind and body. And the third step is to become as unattached to the healing process as to the trauma and go on living a successful life.

There are other general benefits that everyone who completes rebirthing receives. One of the most important is the ability to receive love and have the direct experience of letting it in. During rebirthing, you are physically able to feel the difference between resisting the love and letting it flow in, and touching is not required to get this experience. As a result, people begin to experience more and more bliss in their daily lives without working at it. As a result, the physical body becomes a more pleasurable place to be. When old aches, pains, and tensions are gone forever, even just walking can become orgasmic. Another benefit is the increase in psychic awareness. Rebirthed people have more and more experiences of telepathy and intuitive knowledge, which again makes life more effortless, fun, and interesting.

In addition to a healthier, more relaxed body, people experience a great deal more physical energy and less need to sleep. The energy formerly used to keep the birth trauma suppressed is released and available for other and better things. As a result, rebirthed people become more beautiful. A propensity for youthfulness occurs as well as a desire for physical immortality. After one has a breathing release, the ability to breathe freely and uninhibitedly becomes natural. This, of course, leads to less effort while working; and therefore working becomes more like playing, especially when people do the thing they love as a career.

The results of rebirthing are not always rosy. The mood swings of an individual's disposition are sometimes exaggerated. Some people report that after rebirthing they experience their highest highs and lowest lows, which eventually level out into bliss. Some people experience pain and other forms of discomfort which seem to be stimulated by the new internal freedom. It is usually possible to come out of rebirthing in a perpetual state of health and bliss, but the path may sometimes be rocky. On the whole, however, rebirthing is the fastest and most effective technique to higher consciousness that we have experienced. If people experience their birth in rebirthing, they may go on to re-experience various periods of infancy which are wrought with feelings of helplessness and hopelessness.

Genuine spiritual experiences may cause either healings or sickness. Causes and cures of specific symptoms already exist in the personality, and the spiritual energy activates and releases the person from these cause-and-effect relationships. Pure aliveness always transcends the wheel of Karma and yields greater personal freedom.

Rebirthing ultimately raises your self-esteem to a very high level. And when that happens, all areas of your life are affected. Relationships with parents and lovers often change drastically for the better. One of the most gratifying experiences I have ever had involved a woman who had been rebirthed several times bringing her mother from Europe to be rebirthed with her. The mother did not speak any English, but it did not matter. The rebirth went perfectly. The daughter cradled her sobbing mother in her arms and the mother got through to the "other side."

The Rebirthed Person

You can rebirth yourself alone. It is, however, wise, pleasurable and appropriate to form a relationship with a rebirther. A qualified rebirther increases the efficiency and safety of the rebirth experience. Later, after you have had a breathing release, you will be able to rebirth yourself safely without the rebirther present. Leonard worked on his own rebirth for over five years and didn't complete it until he trained a dozen rebirthers and had them rebirth him. His conclusion: Certain aspects, because of the complexity of the mind and the time between birth and rebirth, are frightening to face without the presence of someone who is experienced and capable. Rebirthing is a regression to infancy, and a characteristic of the infant is a need to be cared for. It is not practical to rebirth yourself until you have passed through the infancy stage.

If you are normal and well-adjusted, and if you are willing to take maximum responsibility for your participation in the rebirth, then you will probably be able to wipe out the substance of your birth trauma and its effects in one to five sessions and will establish a new relationship to your divine spiritual energy. If you devote your complete attention and will to the rebirthing, it is easy. If you are essentially unwilling to face the truth about yourself, it may take a hundred sessions to do the same thing. Paradoxically, fear of failure prevents success. A willingness to face things is characteristic of successful people.

Rebirthing can be done in groups, but it is much preferable to do it individually so that you can have all the loving attention that you deserve and did not get in your original birth. Leonard has experimented with doing fifty to a hundred people at once by having them work in pairs. He feels that this is not ideal. However, the results are too beneficial to ignore. Because of my work in loving relationships training, I especially enjoy rebirthing couples. Watching each other go through this process produced a whole new level of understanding and depth of love.

As rebirthing and other forms of spiritual enlightenment become more widespread throughout society, more and more people will be spontaneously induced into a rebirth experience by the psychic safety produced by enlightened people around them. The rebirth phenomenon is totally safe if you just relax and breath in a relaxed manner. A common denominator in birth trauma is fear of irreparable damage. Most people resent leaving the womb and therefore experience irreparable damage in being denied readmission. Since they don't integrate the experience of birth into their consciousness and understand it, they go through life with a constant fear of irreparable damage. Unfortunately the subconscious can take this fear and turn it into a causative expectation. When you study the impact in human emotions of the birth trauma, you can see what it causes everywhere in human behavior. For example, we noted a statistical correlation in people who are slapped on the fanny at birth and people who later have rear ended automobile accidents. Many forms of crime, victim consciousness, failure and illness can be traced to this fear of irreparable damage.

Whenever you experience intense anxiety, fear of harm, or irreparable damage, find a safe place and sit or lie down, relax and breathe. If you are working with a well-trained rebirther, you will quickly understand the dynamics of all this and learn how to handle it with ease.

Rebirth Affirmations

1. I am breathing fully and freely.
2. I survived my birth, therefore my parents and doctor, and I myself, love life more than death and choose my survival.
3. My physical body is a pleasant and wonderful vehicle for my full and free self-expression.
4. I am glad to be out of the womb so I can express myself fully and freely.
5. I now receive assistance and cooperation from people.
6. I am safe, protected by Infinite Intelligence and Infinite Love, people and things no longer hurt me without my conscious permission.
7. I am no longer afraid of my breath.
8. I have the right and ability to express my hostility about my birth without losing people's love and support.
9. I am now willing to see my birth clearly.
10. Feeling all my emptiness won't destroy me.
11. I forgive myself for the pain I caused myself at birth.
12. Energy and vitality are my birthright.
13. My mother loves and appreciates me.
14. My mother is now glad that I was born.
15. My mother is now happy to get me out of the womb.
16. It was a privilege for my mother to have the honor to bring me into the world.
17. I am the way, the truth and the life. I came through her body and I am glad to be here. The entire universe is glad that I am here.
18. I no longer feel unwanted. The universe rejoices at my presence in it.
19. The universe is singing in my atoms.
20. My mother, father, family and friends are all glad that I was born and that I am alive.
21. Praise the Lord for the perfection of my living flesh.

More About Affirmations

Remember, an affirmation is a positive thought that you consciously choose to immerse in your consciousness to achieve a desired result. It is also like a prayer that you impress on Infinite Spirit. Saying an affirmation or writing it is a way of loving yourself. Ultimately, it is a good idea to BECOME an affirmation. Then you are in a constant state of prayer. One day that will happen naturally. In the meantime, you more or less have to train your mind. Saying and writing affirmations is a very spiritual and powerful thing to do; however, it is important to remember that "love brings up anything unlike itself." Since doing affirmations is a way of loving yourself, anything in the way of your having that new result in your life will present itself to be dealt with. At first this may make your life seem rather strange, but if you keep doing the affirmation the resistance will be dissolved, the affirmation will eventually be integrated into your consciousness and the new thought will manifest.

Think positive thoughts about your partner and loved ones. Holding on to negative thoughts about them only fortifies their negatives.

For your pleasure and ease, I now offer you a host of excellent affirmations about relationships.

Affirmations for Relationships

1. I love myself, therefore others love me.
2. I am highly pleasing to myself in the presence of others.
3. I am willing to accept love and stop resisting.
4. It is safe to surrender to love.
5. Love is my safety.
6. I am willing to let myself be supported in love.
7. Love always heals me.
8. I always get what I want and I only want good things for me.
9. I only attract loving, good people.
10. I no longer suppress my feelings. I express my feelings to others easily.
11. I now chose pleasure in my life. Pleasure leads to more pleasure.
12. I love God and I love life; therefore everyone loves me totally.
13. I now have a success consciousness.
14. I forgive my mother for her ignorant behavior toward me.
15. I forgive my father for his ignorant behavior toward me.
16. I am ready to experience compassion, love, and friendship with my parents, no matter where they are.
17. I no longer attract mates who are my parents. I now attract mates in harmony with my highest spiritual thoughts.
18. I forgive myself completely. I am innocent.
19. I no longer need to fail to get even.
20. I am no longer a helpless infant. I love being grown-up and taking responsibility for my creativity.
21. I am willing to let go of the struggle in relationships and allow myself to have an easy, effortless experience.
22. My body is young and healthy and I am healed.
23. It is safe to indulge in all my favorite pleasures in my relationship.
24. The more I pleasure myself, the closer to remembering God I am.

25. I forgive my family for being confused about sex. I forgive them and myself for suppressing sexual feelings.
26. I am willing now for suppressed incestuous feelings to surface safely and pleasurably.
27. My negative patterns are now dissolving effortlessly.
28. Since what I think about expands, I think only about the good things and breathe out the negative things.
29. I love rebirthing myself with my partner and we remember to do this often.
30. My life urges are stronger than my death urges, and as long as I continue to strengthen my life urges and weaken my death urges, I will go on living in health, happiness, and in great relationships.
31. I am now changing my most negative thought about myself to _____.
32. I am now changing my most negative thought on relationships to _____.
33. My partner and I always have and enjoy ever-increasing love, health, happiness, wealth, wisdom, harmony, full self-expression, sexual bliss, and physical immortality.
34. My past is complete. Everything is resolving itself harmoniously.
35. All my past relationships are now clearing up easily and pleasurably.
36. My partner and I give each other abundant psychic space in which we feel comfortable.
87. I now take responsibility for my feelings of jealousy and do not blame it on my state.
38. The more self-esteem I have, the less jealousy I have.
39. My sex life improves daily.
40. Since people treat me the way I treat myself, I am now treating myself fabulously.
41. I am a beautiful lovable person, and I deserve love.
42. Every day, and in every way, I am more and more able to receive.
43. All of my relationships are now loving, lasting, and harmonious.

44. I am always being nourished in my relationships.
45. My communication is always clear and productive in my relationships.
46. I always treat my partner with the utmost kindness.
47. My partner and I easily surrender to the highest spiritual thought.
48. We now always handle our anger in appropriate ways.
49. We both always tell the truth as fast as we can.
50. Every day we express, verbally and physically, more and more love to each other.
51. Our relationship gets more and more exciting every day.
52. Every day and in every way we become closer and closer.
53. Every day our relationship becomes more and more romantic and immortal.
54. Every day we are feeling more passionate and healthier.
55. I give thanks daily for this partner and I acknowledge myself for creating this relationship.
56. My partner and I serve God together and express the Spirit in high fashion by sharing our life and light with the world.
57. Our relationship is filled with joy and fun and miracle consciousness.
58. Our relationship becomes perfect as we become perfect.
59. I can easily create new relationships whenever I want by the power of my mind.
60. The more beautiful my thoughts are, the more beautiful people I attract.

ABOUT THE LRT

The LRT is the Loving Relationships Training. A weekend workshop, this magical gathering empowers you to raise your self-esteem, locate and release unconscious negative patterns, and apply the patterns of spiritual enlightenment towards practical life changes. At the LRT you transform your relationships with yourself, your family, your mate, your body, your career and God. It is unique in that it helps you to see how your birth script influences all your major relationships and how the unconscious death urge can sabotage you without your knowing it. For further information contact LRT International, P.O. Box 1465, Washington, CT 06793, (800) INT'L LRT, (203) 354-8509.